75 Fantastic
PHYSICS FACTS
Every kid should know!

AF658854

ARCTURUS

ARCTURUS
First edition published in 2023 by Arcturus Publishing Limited
26/27 Bickels Yard, 151–153 Bermondsey Street,
London SE1 3HA

Copyright © Arcturus Holdings Limited

Anne Rooney has asserted her right to be identified as the author of this text in accordance with the Copyright, Designs, and Patents Act 1988.

All rights reserved. No part of this publication may be reproduced, stored in a retrieval system, or transmitted, in any form or by any means, electronic, mechanical, photocopying, recording, or otherwise, without prior written permission in accordance with the provisions of the Copyright Act 1956 (as amended). Any person or persons who do any unauthorized act in relation to this publication may be liable to criminal prosecution and civil claims for damages.

Author: Anne Rooney
Illustrator: Nancy Butterworth
Editor: Rebecca Razo
Designer: Stefan Holliland

Published and Distributed in India by Scholastic India Pvt. Ltd.
First edition: 2023
This Reprint Edition: July 2026

ISBN: 978-93-5954-026-9

Printed in India at Shiv Shakti Printing & Trading Co., Haryana

Welcome to the Fantastic World of Physics!

Did you know that the Universe used to be orange?

Or that you weigh more in sunlight than you do in shade?

Or that a cloud can be as heavy as a jumbo jet?

From the mysteries of our vast Universe to the laws of motion, and much, much more, this book is jam-packed with awe-inspiring physics facts that have been especially chosen to astound and amaze you (and some just to make you giggle).

You'll find plenty of interesting facts to ponder and discuss—and you'll be able to impress your friends and family with your science knowledge! Some of the information might even come in handy if, say, you find yourself on the Moon or drifting in the direction of a black hole.

There is no wrong way to use this book. You can start at the beginning and read straight through, or you can skip around and read whatever you find most interesting—the choice is yours. We've also included loads of illustrations. A few are scientific diagrams, but most of them are fun and quirky so you'll laugh while you learn.

Ready to learn some mind-blowing physics facts? Turn the page to get started!

1 A cloud is as heavy as a jumbo jet

We think of clouds as light and airy—as "light as air" even. After all, they float high in the sky (so surely they can't be very heavy). But a cloud is made of a huge number of tiny water droplets—and water is heavier than air.

Making clouds

The air always contains a lot of water vapor—water as a gas—but you can't see it, just as you can't see other gases in the air. Where the air is cold enough, the gas condenses to liquid water, forming droplets around specks of dust, salt, smoke, or any other bit of solid matter in the air. When a large collection of droplets is visible, we see it as a cloud.

Up or down?

While the droplets in a cloud are small, they are held up by rising air beneath and around them. But if the droplets get too big, gravity pulls them down to the Earth. That's when it rains! The droplets are too heavy to stay suspended, so they fall.

If it's really cold, the droplets in a cloud can freeze. Then they might stick together, forming larger, heavier clumps that become too heavy to stay up. This time, they fall as snow.

DID YOU KNOW?

Sometimes a cloud collapses suddenly, dumping all its water in a "cloudburst."

Rain you never feel

In some places, rain even evaporates before it hits the ground. This "phantom rain" falls from the sky, but it never reaches the ground.

2 Sunlight takes more than eight minutes to reach Earth

The Sun is so far away at 150 million km (93 million mi) that it takes about eight minutes and 20 seconds for sunlight to travel through space to Earth.

Light travels very fast, but it's a long way from the Sun to the Earth. That also means that if the Sun exploded (don't worry, it can't!), we wouldn't know for more than eight minutes.

DID YOU KNOW?

Nothing can ever travel faster than the speed of light. There seems to be a speed limit set on the entire Universe.

Speeding along

Light and other electromagnetic radiation, such as radio waves and microwaves, travel through space at nearly 300,000 km (186,000 mi) per second. That means when you're looking at something on Earth, you see it instantly, but when you look at things in space, they're so far away the light takes a measurable amount of time to get here. Astronomers measure huge distances in space in "light years," which is the distance light can travel in one year: 9 trillion km (6 trillion mi). The next-nearest star is 4.2 light years away, which means the light takes 4.2 years to reach us.

Listening in

Other types of electromagnetic radiation travel at the same speed as light. That means that our radio and television broadcasts that have been leaking out into space for more than 100 years could possibly be picked up by aliens up to 100 light years away—if they have the right equipment.

3 Lightning makes the air explode

Lightning carries a huge amount of electric current from a storm cloud to the ground. The electricity heats up the air it passes through to such a high temperature the air around it actually explodes, making a loud bang that we hear as thunder.

Negative and positive

Electricity flows as tiny negatively charged particles called electrons. If you make a circuit using a battery, electrons flow around the circuit from the negative terminal (end) of the battery to the positive terminal. Similar charges repel (push away) each other, so a negative charge tries to stay away from another negative charge. Opposite charges are attracted to each other.

Sky to ground

The bottom part of a storm cloud builds up a strong negative electric charge, which pushes away the negatively charged electrons on the ground. That gives the ground a positive charge. The electrons in the cloud are then attracted to the positive charge pooled in the ground.

Lightning starts with a small negative charge from a cloud taking short "steps" in the direction of the ground of about 50 m (164 ft) each. Each step takes less than a millionth of a second. When it gets close to the ground, streams of positive electric charge from the ground leap up to meet it, making a complete path. At this point, the cloud pours out its negative electric charge. The air is heated so quickly it expands rapidly, exploding with a flash. Thunder is the shock wave from the explosion, which we hear as sound.

4 A huge star will soon explode

The star Betelgeuse is likely to self-destruct in a massive explosion called a supernova some time in the next few hundred thousand years.

It could be tomorrow and at 650 light years away, it's kind of close. Fortunately, it's far enough away not to hurt us. Phew!

Running out of gas

All stars spend their life squashing hydrogen into helium, releasing energy as heat and light, x-rays, microwaves, and other forms of radiation. This is called nuclear fusion, and it's how stars make light and heat. When they run out of hydrogen, they fuse the helium into larger atoms, and those into even larger atoms, up to iron. Then they're stuck, as it takes too much energy to force iron atoms together to make anything else.

Collapse!

While the star is working normally, it's stable. The pressure of energy streaming out balances gravity pulling in. When there's nothing pushing out, though, gravity wins and pulls all parts of the star toward the middle. But there's no room in the middle, so the star explodes and its bits are hurled out into space. The remains are a growing, glowing cloud of gas and dust that can be seen for thousands of years.

5 The Sun is middle-aged

The Sun has been shining for 4.6 billion years, and it's got enough hydrogen to keep going for about another 5 billion years—so we don't need to worry just yet.

The largest stars have the shortest lives. Medium-sized stars like the Sun keep going for several billion years. Smaller stars, called red dwarfs, last much longer—possibly trillions of years. The Universe is not old enough for any of them to have died yet. Additionally, our Sun is too small to explode.

6 You can measure the tallest tree with a short ruler

As long as the Sun is shining, you can measure the height of a tall tree or building from the length of its shadow.

How tall are you?

You might have noticed that the length of your shadow changes. In the middle of the day, when the Sun is nearly overhead, your shadow is short. In the early morning or evening, when the Sun is low in the sky, your shadow is longer. The same is true of the shadows of things around you. The ratio of your height to your shadow changes during the day, but at any moment the ratio will be the same for all objects that cast a shadow. So when your shadow is half as long as your height, the shadow of a tree will be half as long as its height. By measuring your own shadow, you can discover the ratio. You can then measure the tree's shadow to work out the height of the tree.

Where's the Sun?

The length of a shadow depends on the angle at which sunlight falls on an object. When the Sun is overhead, there is a wide angle between the Sun and the ground. When it's low, there is a small angle. The angle of the Sun in relation to where you are changes as Earth rotates.

7 Potatoes are electric

Or at least, you can get electricity from potatoes!

Using two potatoes, two zinc-coated nails, and some copper wire, you can generate an electric current and use the potatoes like a battery.

Acid, potatoes, and electricity

A battery produces electricity from a chemical reaction. One terminal of the battery releases electrons that travel to the other terminal, creating a current.

You can make a potato battery by sticking a zinc nail in one end of the potato and a copper wire in the other end. Acid in the potato attacks the zinc and frees some electrons, which travel to the copper wire. If you connect two potatoes together, linking the nail on one potato to the copper wire on another with insulated wire, and then connect the other terminals to a small clock or low-voltage bulb, you can use the electricity generated by the potatoes.

Positive?

Electrons are freed from zinc in a chemical reaction with the acid in the potato. The zinc acts as the negative terminal, or anode, in the electric circuit, providing electrons. They travel to the copper wire, which acts as a cathode, or positive terminal, in the circuit. The electrons travel through the connecting wire between the potatoes and the bulb, or clock. The potatoes work as an electrochemical cell, converting the chemical energy of a reaction into electricity.

Running out of potato juice

Your potato battery won't last very long—the potato doesn't contain many of the chemicals, called electrolytes, needed to make electricity.

8 The stars are still there in the daytime

At night, we can see the stars and Moon, and in the daytime we can see the Sun (and sometimes the Moon, too). But the stars don't go away in the daytime—they are still there, in the same places. The Sun's light is so bright, though, that we aren't able to see the stars.

A whole sky of stars

As Earth turns around on its axis, the place you are on the planet sometimes faces the Sun. Other times, it faces out into the darkness of space. When it faces the Sun, it's day. When it faces away from the Sun, it's night. There are stars all around the Earth, so you will always be facing some stars, even when you can't see them.

As Earth goes around the Sun over the course of a year, your bit of Earth faces different parts of the sky at different times. That's why you might see different stars in summer and winter, or why some might appear in different places in the sky.

Too bright

When your part of Earth is facing the Sun, the Sun is so bright that you can't see any other stars It lights up the whole sky, swamping starlight. But we sometimes get a peek at stars during daylight A total eclipse happens when the Moon passes directly between Earth and the Sun. Its shadow blots out the Sun and the sky goes dark in the middle of the day. Then you can see the daytime stars for a few minutes!

9 Some stones float on water

Pumice is a spongy rock full of bubbles. It has hardened from frothy molten rock that has come from volcanoes. Because of all the air bubbles, it is less dense than water and it floats.

Hot sponges!

When a volcano erupts, scalding hot molten rock (called lava) and a lot of gas pour from deep inside Earth. All the gas mixed into the molten rock can make for a very explosive eruption, with lava hurled into the air with great force. Once it's outside in the air, the rock quickly cools and hardens. It's still full of bubbles, so it looks like a sponge.

Sink or float?

Whether something sinks or floats depends on its density.

Density is the mass of a fixed volume of a substance. A cube of water measuring 1 cm along each side (1 cm^3) has a mass of one gram. If something has lower density than water, 1 cm^3 will have a mass of less than one gram and it will float. If it has a higher density than water, 1 cm^3 will have a mass of more than one gram and it will sink. Wood is less dense than water, and it floats. Metal is more dense than water, and it sinks. A piece of pumice stone is made of rock that is more dense than water, but it has lots of holes filled with air or other gases. Air is less dense than water. Pumice is overall less dense than water, so it floats. After a volcanic eruption near the sea, there are often thousands of pumice pebbles floating on the water.

10 In space, no one can hear you scream

Sound travels as waves, but is carried as vibrations in atoms. That means it needs to be carried by a medium—or a substance—such as air or water. In space, where there is no air, there is nothing to vibrate and therefore nothing to carry sound. It's eerily silent, no matter what happens.

Shaking sounds

Sound is produced by something vibrating, which then makes the air molecules around it vibrate. If you bang a drum, the skin of the drum vibrates, and that sets the molecules in the air closest to it vibrating. Their vibrations are passed on to the next nearest molecules, and so on, spreading out in waves.

DID YOU KNOW?

The Big Bang that formed the Universe nearly 13.8 billion years ago was silent. We don't know what it was like, but it couldn't have made a noise, as there was nothing to carry sound energy.

Listen, hear

You can hear sounds because the vibrating air molecules make molecules in your ear vibrate. The vibrations are passed on through the parts of your ear until they are converted into signals to send to your brain, which interprets the sounds. If you were in space, nothing could make a sound and you couldn't hear anything except what's happening in your own body. Even something you would expect to be really loud, like a star exploding in a supernova, would be silent.

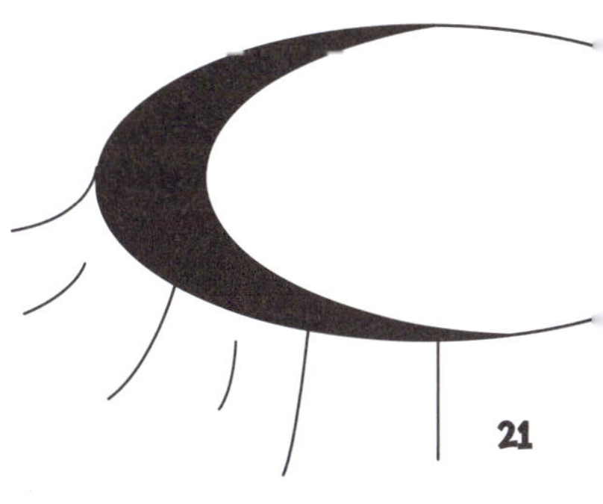

11 An echo is a reflected noise

Have you ever stood in a cave or tunnel and shouted, only to hear your shout repeated to you in an echo? The sound of your voice bounces off the walls and comes back to you, like a reflection.

Reflecting light and sound

When you look in a mirror you see your reflection immediately; you don't have to wait for it. But sound travels more slowly than light, so there's a bit of a pause.

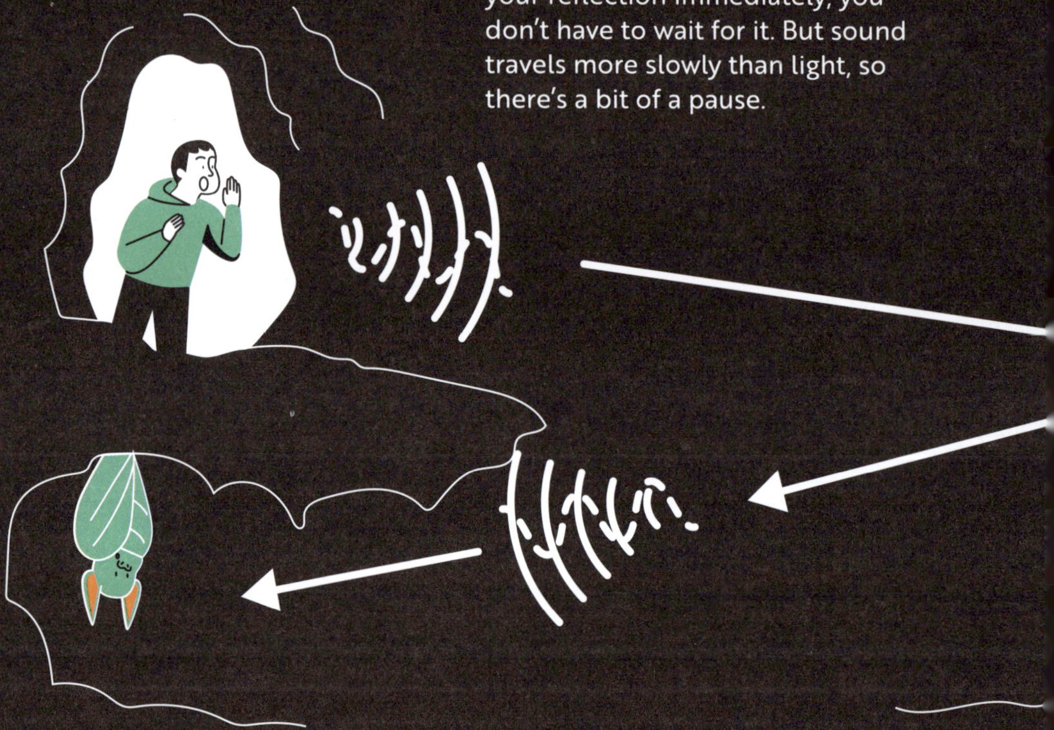

Wavy sounds

Sound travels as waves, carried as vibrations in the substance it moves through. In air, the vibrations travel at 343 m per second (1,125 ft per second). When they reach a solid surface, such as a brick wall or stone cliff face, the vibrations bounce back off. They keep the same pattern, so the sound is the same. If you're surrounded by hard surfaces, the echo itself might be reflected, so then you hear it several times.

12 Aliens might be able to see dinosaurs

An alien on a planet 66 million light years away would see light that left the solar system 66 million years ago. If it had a telescope good enough to see detail on Earth's surface, it might see dinosaurs!

When you look at a distant star, you're seeing light that left it thousands of years ago. Looking at the stars, we are watching the past. It's the same for any aliens that might be looking at our Sun or the Earth.

13 Ice can crush a ship without moving

If a ship stops moving at a place where water is freezing, the ice can crush the ship as it freezes around it. This happened to the explorer Ernest Shackleton's ship Endurance in Antarctica in 1915—fortunately, everyone on the ship survived the event.

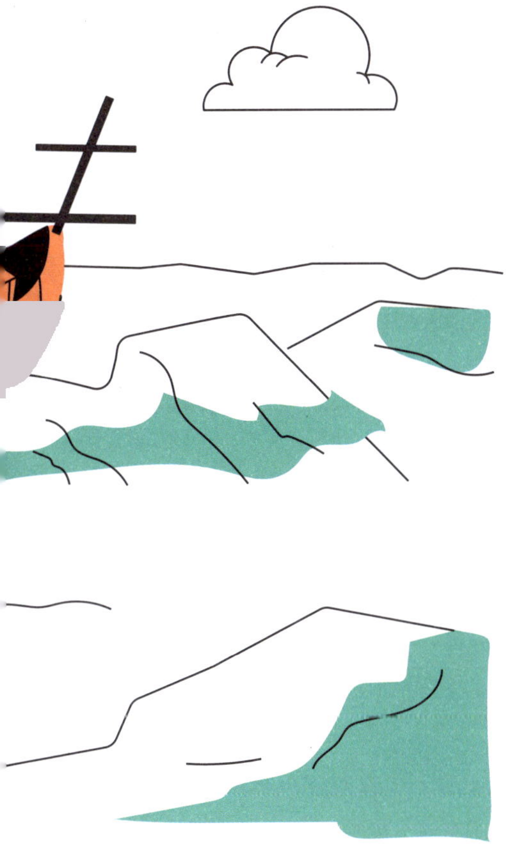

Expanding ice

Most substances shrink as they freeze from liquid to solid, but water is very unusual in that it expands (takes up more space) as it solidifies. This is why ice floats on water—it's less dense than water, meaning the same mass has a greater volume. That's great because it means you can float ice in your drinks! It's less great if you're sailing a wooden ship into an ice field.

When a ship is in a clear space of water surrounded by ice, and the temperature is dropping, more of the sea freezes, closing the gap between the ship and surrounding ice. But as the ice takes up more space than the water did, it doesn't just freeze up to the edge of the ship and stop. The increasing volume of the ice needs the space the ship is occupying. Whereas water will flow around an object, ice does not. The pack ice builds up at the edges of the ice sheet. One molecule at a time, the ice creeps up on the ship's space, slowly crushing it with immense force. The ice isn't moving, but it's growing. It's a slow, cold death for the ship.

14 If an atom were the size of a sports stadium, electrons would be like bees

An atom is the smallest particle of matter that can be said to be a single substance—one of the chemical elements, such as gold or oxygen. Each atom has a nucleus in the middle, and electrons that whiz around it in a cloud.

Inside an atom

An atom is made of three types of particle: neutrons and protons in the nucleus, and electrons. Although the electrons "belong" with the nucleus, they don't stay close to it.

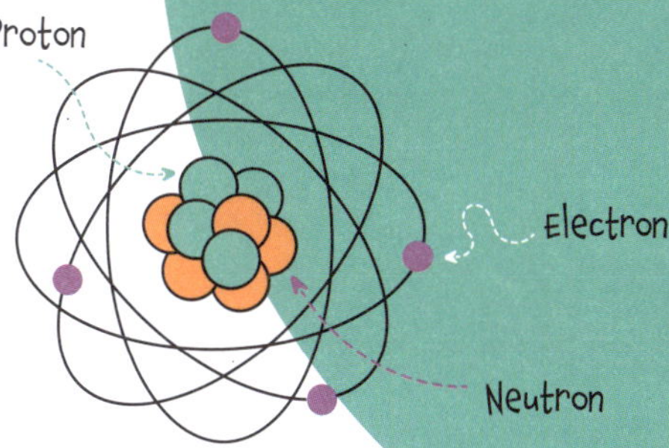

In orbit

An atom is a bit like an onion with layers, called orbits, that can each have a set number of electrons. More electrons take more layers. So an atom with lots of electrons—like gold, which has 79 electrons—is bigger than one with just a few electrons, like carbon, which has just six.

Tiny middle, lots of space

The nucleus of an atom takes up only about one ten-thousandth of its width, yet contains almost all the mass. Electrons are a tiny part of the mass of an atom—the nucleus Is about 3,600 times as heavy as the electrons. The size of the whole atom is set by the space that the electrons can move around in, and they can go a long way out. If the nucleus of an average atom were the size of an apple, some of its electrons would be about 2 km (1.2 mi) away!

15 Most of your body is as old as the Universe

Your body is made up of lots of different chemicals, and those are made mostly from just a few elements: hydrogen, carbon, oxygen, nitrogen, phosphorous, and sulfur. These make up 99 percent of your body.

The nuclei (middles) of the hydrogen atoms were all made within a few minutes of the Universe starting in the Big Bang.

You're recycled

There's hydrogen in lots of different chemicals in your body, including water, fats, carbohydrates, and the DNA that carries your genetic information.

Every one of those hydrogen atoms has had an exciting journey on its way to you. From just whirling around in space, an atom might then have been in one or more stars for a while. After getting snaffled up into the growing Earth 4.55 billion years ago, it's probably been through rocks, oceans, clouds, and lots of other organisms, including dinosaurs, deep-sea creatures, and plants. After you've finished with your hydrogen atoms, they'll be recycled again into something else.

16 You're made from stars

The rest of the atoms in your body were made in stars, or in the catastrophic explosions of dying stars: supernovas. Stars squash together hydrogen atoms to make helium, and then squash helium together to make larger atoms, and so on. When a star finally dies, everything it has made gets thrown out into space. Then it can be swept up in newly forming stars and planets, and eventually built into rocks, or plants, or people.

17 The Moon is upside down at the South Pole

Or, if you live in the Southern Hemisphere, it looks upside down at the North Pole. Whichever way up the Moon looks to you, it looks the other way at the other end (top or bottom) of the world.

No, you're upside down!

The Moon rotates on its axis—an imaginary line drawn through it from top to bottom. It doesn't "roll over," top to bottom. But how the Moon looks depends on where you are standing on Earth to look at it. From the North Pole, you look at the Moon like this:

From the South Pole, you see it like this because you're now "upside down," compared to someone at the North Pole.

Poles apart?

Most people don't see the Moon from the North Pole or the South Pole but from somewhere in between, so the Moon is a bit more sideways. If you stood right on the equator, the Moon would look as though it had been tipped over through 90 degrees from the view at either pole.

18 The Moon's phases go the wrong way in the other hemisphere

If you're in the Northern Hemisphere, a waxing crescent Moon is a curve of Moon on the right as you look at it. But if you're in the Southern Hemisphere, the crescent is on the left—the Moon's phases are reversed. If you're at the equator, the crescent lies at the bottom. Again, it's not the Moon—it's you!

19 You can't make a decent snowman on a ski slope

Some snow is good for snowball fights and making snowmen; other snow is good for skiing and sledging. If it's good for one, it's not good for the other.

Big and small, wet and dry

Snow can be "wet" or "dry." Wet snow has large flakes that can quickly create a deep layer of snow. Large flakes form in slightly warmer air (0–2°C / 32–35°F). It's warm enough for the edges of small ice crystals to melt and stick together, so small flakes form clumps that become big flakes. The wetness makes it easy for you to stick snow together to make a snowman.

When small flakes fall through colder air, they don't melt and stick together. These fall as powdery snow. If the air temperature remains below the freezing point of water at 0°C (32°F), this snow stays frozen on the ground, so it's great for winter sports.

Slow and steady

Snowflakes fall at about 1.6–6.4 kph (1–4 mph) depending on their size and the conditions around them. The average speed is about 2.4 kph (1.5 mph). That means it takes a snowflake about an hour to fall from a cloud to the ground.

Really unique?

It's said that every snowflake has its own unique design. This can't be proven one way or another, but the way snowflakes form, by tiny crystals sticking together, means there is plenty of chance for them to be different.

20 The USA is wider than Pluto

The dwarf planet Pluto really is small: Its diameter is just over half the width of the USA. The total surface area of Pluto is still larger than the land area of the USA, but less than twice the size at 17.7 million km^2 (6.8 million sq mi) for Pluto and 9.8 million km^2 (3.8 million sq mi) for the USA.

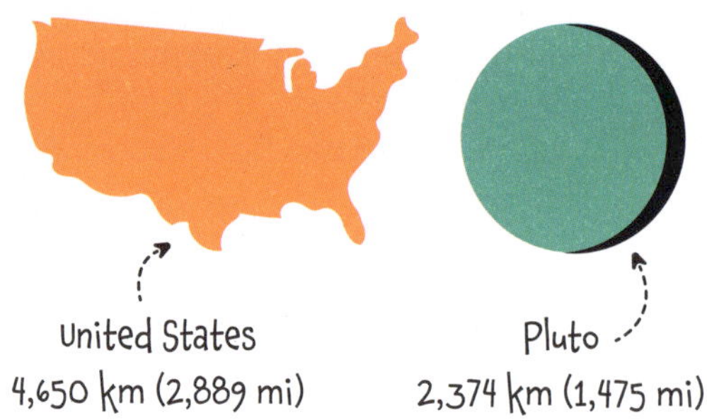

Once a planet...

Pluto was once classed as a planet, but it was downgraded to "dwarf planet" in 2006. It was always the smallest planet, but the International Astronomical Union brought in new rules for planets, and Pluto didn't make the grade.

A planet must:

- orbit the Sun,
- be round or nearly round, and
- have cleared its own orbit by sweeping up any other matter circling in its path.

Pluto failed the last test. It's in a part of space called the Kuiper Belt, with lots of other objects. Because many other objects share Pluto's orbit, Pluto can no longer be a planet.

Sweeping the sky

The qualifications for being a planet are all related to gravity. Gravity holds planets in orbit around the Sun. A planet's own gravity pulls on all parts of its surface and interior, making the planet round if it has enough mass (and so enough gravity). It clears its orbit by dragging in and absorbing any extra bits and pieces in its path. If it doesn't have enough mass/gravity, it can't do this, so it can't earn its planet badge.

21 White light hides a rainbow

When the Sun shines through rain, you can sometimes see a rainbow: a full spectrum from red to violet. All that brilliance is hidden in sunlight.

White light is a mix of light of different colors, and it can be split apart. We can do it with a block of glass, called a prism, or we can wait for a rainbow. When light moves between substances, such as from air to glass or water, it is refracted, or sent off course a bit. Light of different colors is refracted by different amounts, splitting white light into a spectrum.

How rainbows are made

Sunlight is refracted as it enters a raindrop; then the beams of light are reflected off the back surface of the raindrop. Finally, they're refracted again as they leave the raindrop, spreading out to make a rainbow.

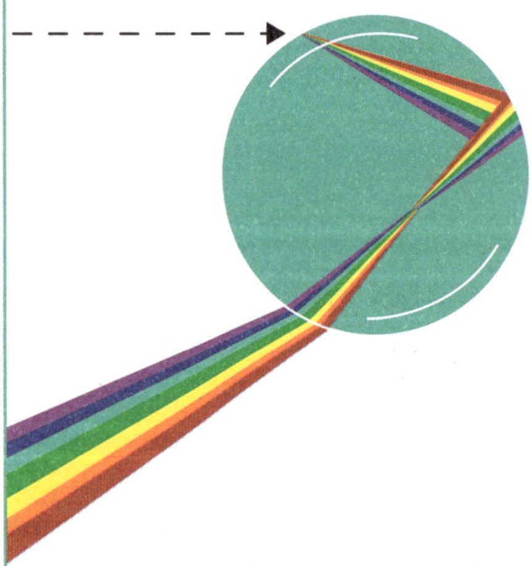

DID YOU KNOW?

You can only see a rainbow when the Sun is behind you.

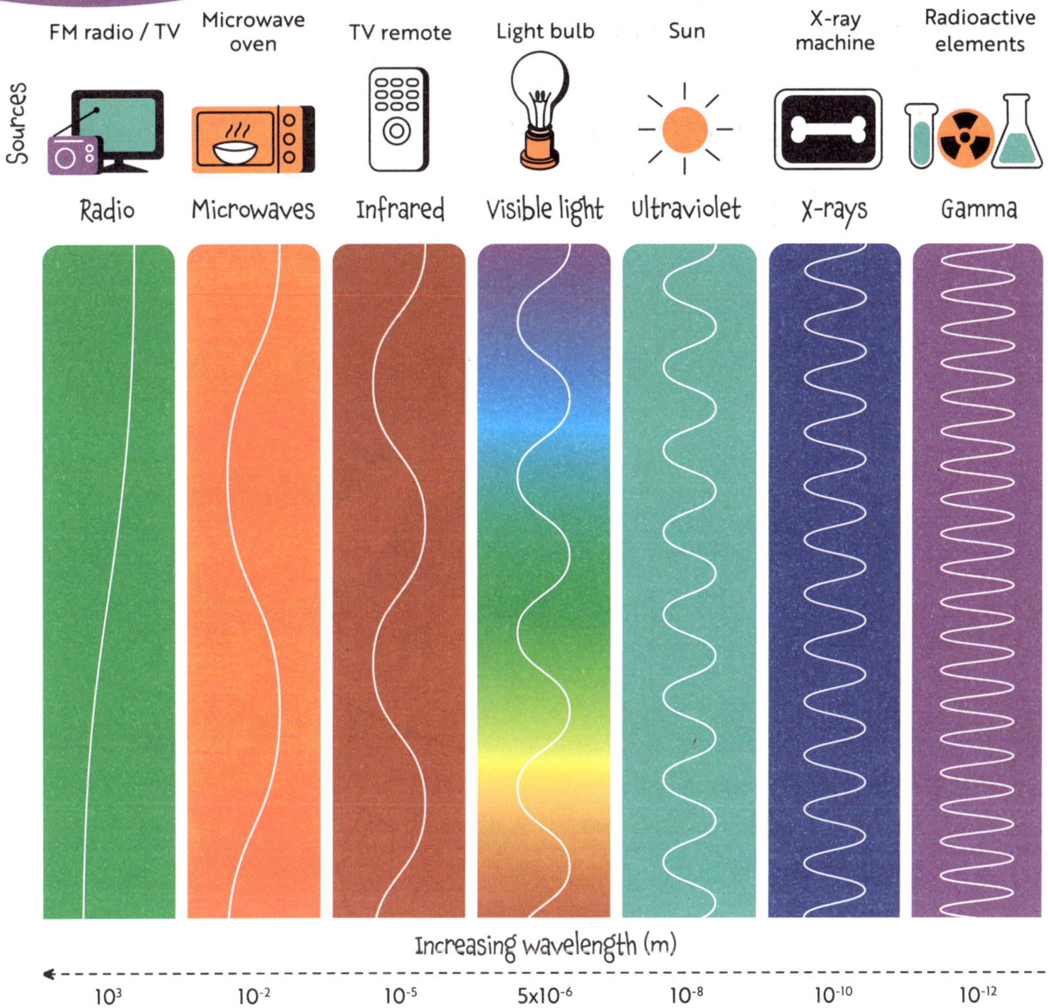

At the energy café

Visible light is part of a whole range of energy that exists as waves, called the electromagnetic spectrum. The length of the waves (their wavelength), sets how the energy behaves. At long wavelengths, it becomes radio waves. We use these for telecommunications, carrying signals for radio, TV, and cell phones. If the wavelength is a bit shorter, it's microwaves, which we can use to heat food. A bit shorter and we see it as light, different wavelengths making different colors. Next come x-rays, which we use to look inside bodies in hospitals and bags at the airport. The shortest are gamma rays, which are dangerous radioactive rays.

22 If you had a long enough lever, you could lift an elephant!

How? An elephant is very heavy. You couldn't pick it up in your arms. But with a lever, you get superpowers!

This simple machine has two parts—a long board, or bar, and a fulcrum.

A lever can be as simple as a plank of wood balanced on a rock. The point where it balances is called the pivot, or fulcrum. When you push down on one side, the other side goes up. It works by magnifying (making bigger) the force you use. To lift your elephant, slide one end of the plank under the elephant, and push down on the other end.

But you'll need a very long plank! If you push down with a force equal to one hundredth of an elephant's mass, you'll need 100 times as much plank on your side as on the elephant's side.

Simple machines

We use levers all the time. If you use a spoon to pry open a tin of cocoa, you're using the spoon as a lever. Playing on a seesaw is playing with a lever!

A lever is one of the six "simple machines" that have been built into all the complicated machinery we have today. The others are a pulley, screw, wedge, inclined plane (sloping surface), and a wheel with an axle.

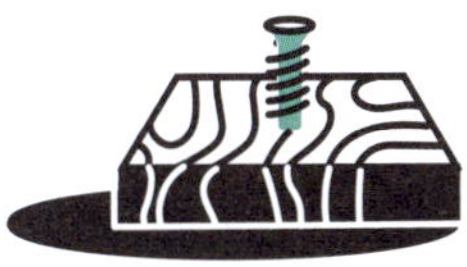

Screw

Let's twist again! This machine turns a circular motion into a movement in one direction.

Pulley

A pulley is a wheel that carries a rope or chain. It shifts energy from one place to another.

Inclined plane

Is a slope really a machine? Well, yes, because it allows objects to be raised more easily.

Wedge

A wedge transforms a forward or downward push into sideways force.

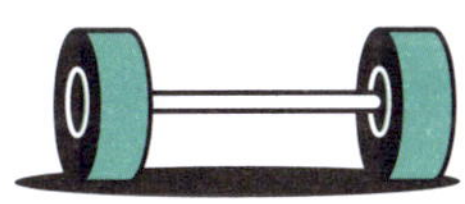

Wheel with axle

This machine's turning motion lets you move an object in a straight line.

Who said that?

The Greek thinker Archimedes is reported to have said, "If you give me a lever and somewhere to stand, I can move the world." In theory it's true, but where would you stand?

23 The far side of the Moon was hidden until 1959

No one and nothing on Earth had ever seen the far side of the Moon until the Soviet spacecraft Luna 3 sent back photographs of it.

Locked in view

The Moon is tidally locked with Earth, so the same side always faces Earth. The Moon orbits Earth once every 27.3 days, and at the same time Earth turns on its own axis. The Moon turns on its axis at the same rate as it orbits Earth, so each day on the Moon lasts a month. On the Moon, around 14 Earth days of darkness are followed by 14 days of light. The result of the Moon's rotation and orbit taking the same amount of time is that only just over half the Moon's surface ever faces Earth, with the other side always facing out into space.

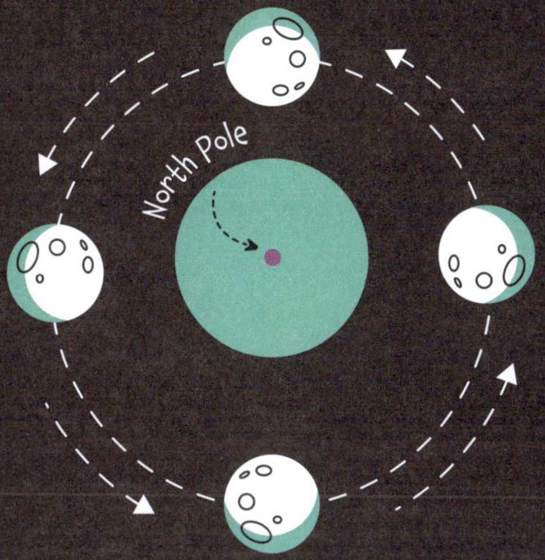

No eyes to see

It's not just humans that had never seen the far side of the Moon. The Moon and Earth have been tidally locked since shortly after the formation of the Moon, 4.5 billion years ago. If there was anything living before tidal locking it was only microbes, which have no eyes. We remain the only beings on Earth ever to see the far side of the Moon. Of course, aliens might have seen it at anytime in the last 4.5 billion years.

DID YOU KNOW?

Only 24 people have ever seen the far side of the Moon in real life. They were all Apollo astronauts who went on a spacecraft that orbited the Moon.

24 The shortest distance between points can be a curve

You're probably used to thinking the shortest distance between two points is a straight line, but if you're journeying over the globe the shortest route is really a curve.

Flat maps and globes

We're used to seeing flat (two-dimensional) maps of Earth. But Earth is really a three-dimensional, slightly squashed sphere. If you drew what seems like a straight line between two points on a globe—say, Sydney and Paris—and then somehow peeled the surface off to make it flat, your line would be curved. It's an arc: a straight line over a curved surface! And if you curved a flat map around a globe, you would find that the straight-line route is actually farther than the arc.

25 Red-hot things aren't that hot

We think of something red-hot as really hot, but red things are the coolest of glowing objects. Really hot objects glow white hot; slightly cooler objects glow yellow.

Glowing hot

Hot objects glow because moving electrons in the object let out little bursts of energy in the form of photons (see page 67). Much of this energy is let out as infrared radiation, which we feel as heat. If they have more energy, they also produce visible light. Red light has the lowest energy of all visible light and is produced first. As something gets hotter, it releases some energy as yellow light, and then other colors. As mixing all the spectrum together produces white light, an object producing light across the spectrum glows white.

26 You'd never have a birthday on Neptune

On Earth, you have a birthday every 365 days, which is once a year. On Neptune, each year is 165 Earth-years long. You wouldn't live long enough to have a birthday if you lived there!

Round and round

Each planet in the solar system goes around the Sun, but they take different amounts of time to do it. The planets closest to the Sun have less distance to travel to go all the way around, so it doesn't take them very long. Mercury, the closest planet, completes its year in just 88 days. When you are 10 on Earth, you would be 42 on Mercury, and you could live to be 300 to 400 Mercury-years old!

A day is the time it takes a planet to turn once on its axis. For Earth, it's 24 hours, but other planets turn at different rates. Neptune turns more quickly and has only 16 hours, 6 ½ minutes in its day. In a Neptune year, there are 40,372 Neptune days.

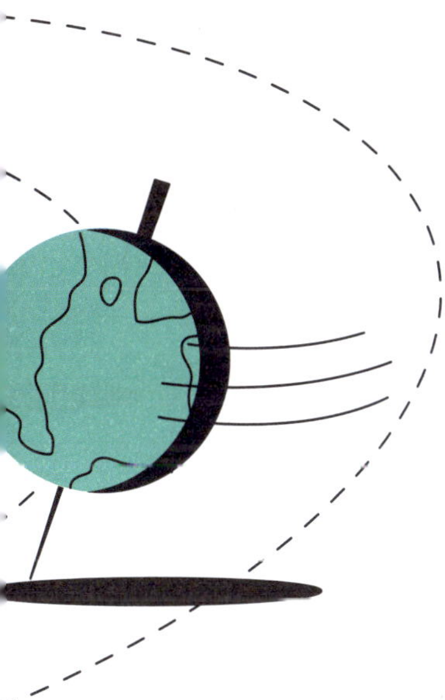

Fast and near

The speed at which a planet goes around the Sun depends on its distance from the Sun. Those closer to the Sun are more affected by its gravity and travel fastest. Mercury moves through space at 48 km (30 mi) per second! Earth orbits at 30 km (19 mi) per second, but Neptune crawls around at only 5 km (3 mi) per second. It sounds slow, but it's still 18,000 km (11,000 mi) per hour. At that speed, you could go all around Earth in just over two hours.

27 Earth is a giant magnet

The middle of Earth, called the core, is made of metal—mostly iron. It has two layers, with a solid inner core and a liquid, molten outer core. Earth turns on its axis, making one full turn every day. As it does, the movement of the liquid metal around the solid core creates a gigantic magnetic field.

Pole to pole

Every magnet has poles, which are where the magnetic field starts and ends. Confusingly, Earth's magnetic poles don't match the places we call the North Pole and the South Pole—and they aren't even positioned at the same ends of the globe! The magnetic north pole is in the south, in Antarctica. The magnetic south pole is in the north, in Canada. The north pole of one magnet always attracts the south pole of another, and that's why the "north" arrow on a compass points north—because it's attracted to Earth's magnetic south pole.

Magnetic protection

Earth's magnetic field stretches millions of miles into space. It's weaker than the magnetism of a fridge magnet, yet strong enough to make the charged particles of the solar wind flow around Earth rather than bombarding us. Without this protective magnetic cloak, the atmosphere would be stripped away and we couldn't live here. Mars has lost both its magnetic field and most of its atmosphere.

28 You can see Earth's magnetic field

Well, you can see its effects. The northern and southern lights are patterns of swirling greens, blues, and pinks seen in the night sky near the North Pole and the South Pole. They are created by Earth's magnetic field interacting with particles in the solar wind, which is the continuous flow of charged particles from the Sun that travels through the solar system.

29 You can weigh things with just water

If you have a measuring jug marked with units of water volume, you can calculate the weight of any object that floats. The mass of water displaced (moved aside) by an object is the same as the mass of the object.

But how much does the water weigh?

In the metric system of measures, 1 cm^3 of water at room temperature weighs 1 gram (g). So if you have a jug containing, say, 200 cm^3 of water and you drop in an apple weighing 100 g, the level of water in the jug will rise to 300 cm^3. The water weighs 200 g, and the apple weighs 100 g. It works because the object is held up by a force called buoyancy, and the force is equal to the weight of the object. The same principal applies to the imperial system of measures. You can also measure how much water overflows if you put an object into a container completely filled with water.

Sinking without a trace

If an object is denser than water, it sinks completely. It displaces its own volume of water, but this time you can't tell its weight. An object can't displace more than its own volume. A stone of 1 cm^3 will displace as much water as a lump of lead of 1 cm^3, but the lead is heavier!

Staying afloat

On ships, a Plimsoll line shows how far up the side of the ship the water comes when the ship is fully loaded. It uses displacement to show when the ship has as much weight as it can safely carry.

30 All the people on Earth could fit into a sugar cube

They wouldn't still be people, but if you removed all the empty space in them, the leftover bits could fit into a cube with sides of about 1 cm (0.6 in).

Mostly nothing

All matter is made of atoms, which have a nucleus in the middle, with one or more electrons going around it. But the electrons are a long way from the nucleus, so most of an atom is empty space (see page 27). Then there's a lot of space between atoms. If you could suck out all that nothing, squashing the parts of atoms really close together, all the humans on Earth really would fit into a tiny cube—but it would still have the same mass as all the people, which is about 500 billion kg!

If we didn't bother to suck out all the space, but could fit all the people together with no gaps between them, the cube would be about 800 m (0.5 mi) along each side—smaller than you would expect!

Holding it together

The nucleus has a positive charge and the electrons all have a negative charge. The electrons naturally push each other away, and stay as far apart as they can. But they are all rattracted to the positive nucleus. It's a tricky balancing act. Do they run away entirely and escape into space? Or do they rush to the attractive middle? They actually keep their distance from each other, but they stay as close as they can to the nucleus. Their balancing act puts all the space in an atom.

31 Saturn would float in the bath

Saturn is a gas giant planet, and it's made of hydrogen and helium, which are light chemicals. This makes the whole planet less dense than water—so it would float if there were a bath big enough to put it in.

States of matter

Matter usually exists in one of three states: solid, liquid, or gas, depending on the temperature and pressure. On Earth, water exists as ice (solid), water (liquid), or gas (water vapor). It moves between states as it's heated or cooled. Heating provides energy to atoms so then they move about more. In a solid, they're held in a fixed place and can only vibrate, but if heated enough, they break free of the solid structure and flow—that's when a solid melts to become liquid. In a gas, the atoms have even more energy and move freely and vigorously, spreading far apart. We can turn a gas back into a liquid or a liquid back into a solid by cooling it, or by putting it under great pressure—squashing it so that the atoms are close together and can't move far. The gas in a gas cylinder is stored as a liquid, under pressure.

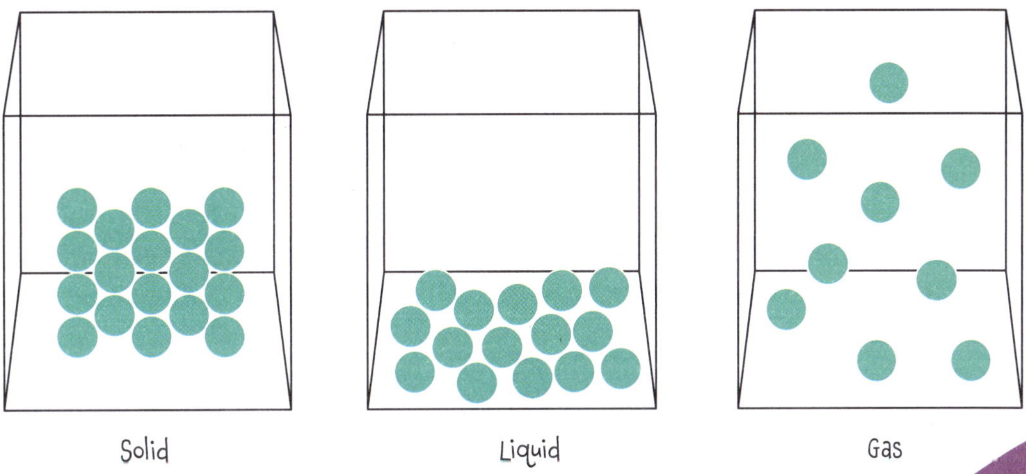

Forced together

Saturn doesn't have a solid surface like Earth does, but the gas becomes thicker and thicker toward the middle until it's liquid, and then a kind of thick slushy ice. This is because the planet's gravity pulls the gas in, creating intense pressure.

32 You can watch molecules move

Molecules are really small. So small that a teaspoon of water holds more than 150,000,000,000,000,000,000,000 (that's 150 million quadrillion) molecules. You wouldn't expect to see something so small moving around ... and you certainly can't with the naked eye or a magnifying glass. But with a microscope, you can watch the *effects* of them moving.

Jostled and nudged

The molecules in a drop of water are moving all the time. When the biologist Robert Brown looked at flower pollen through his microscope in 1827, he was surprised to see bits jiggling around as though they could move on their own. In fact, as Einstein explained 80 years later, the pollen was being jostled by the moving water molecules. As molecules crashed into the bits of pollen, they pushed and shoved them around. Brown couldn't see the molecules themselves, but he could see the movement they caused.

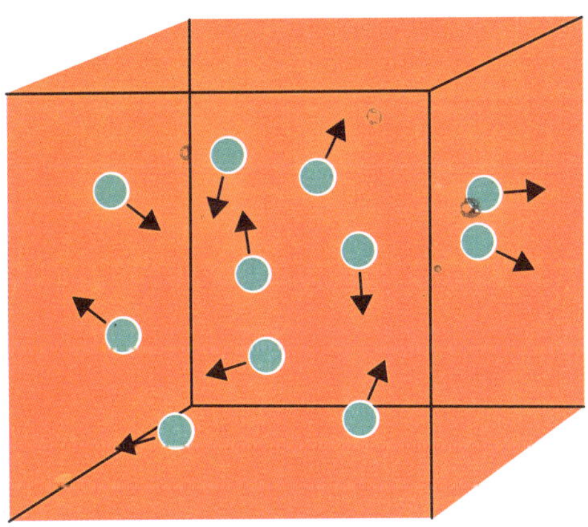

On the move

Molecules and atoms in a liquid or gas are moving all the time. They produce pressure when they push against a solid surface, whether that's the edge of a container or something floating around in it.

What Brown saw through his microscope was the result of pollen being bombarded by millions of water molecules at the same time, coming from all directions. The molecules move in a random way, and the pollen grains were buffeted from all directions. Just by chance, sometimes they were pushed more one way than another, so they moved a bit. Scientists soon discovered it wasn't only pollen that was jostled around like this, but any tiny particles held in water.

33 Even the brightest Moon produces no light

The Moon and planets don't make any light of their own. They only shine with reflected sunlight. The rocky planets and the Moon are made of rock, and the gas planets are made of gas and ice—neither of these can produce light.

Bright white

When sunlight falls onto the surface of a moon or planet, some of it is reflected. The paler the surface, the more light is reflected. The Moon is made of pale grey rock, so it reflects a lot of light and looks bright white. The Moon has dark patches on it, though. These are areas of different rock that reflect less light. Enceladus, a moon of Saturn, is entirely covered in ice. It's so white it reflects 90 percent of the sunlight that falls on it.

It's all in the light

White and pale objects reflect most of the light that falls on them. But many other objects reflect light in just one part of the spectrum and absorb other wavelengths of light. Light of different wavelengths appears as different hues. We can only see the light that bounces back to us from an object. An object that absorbs all light except red light will look red to us, as it reflects only red light. An object that absorbs all light except blue light will look blue. And an object that absorbs all light will look black, as it's not reflecting any light at all.

34 Heat can burst a balloon

Don't put your balloon near a heater if you don't want it to burst!

A balloon will burst if it gets too hot. Raising the temperature increases the pressure inside the balloon until it's too great for the skin of the balloon to contain, and the balloon bursts.

Under pressure

When you blow up a balloon, its thin skin of rubber, or plastic, stretches and the balloon expands to hold the air you blow in. The rubber resists stretching, so the air inside the balloon is at a higher pressure than the air outside the balloon. This means there are more gas molecules in the same volume inside the balloon than outside.

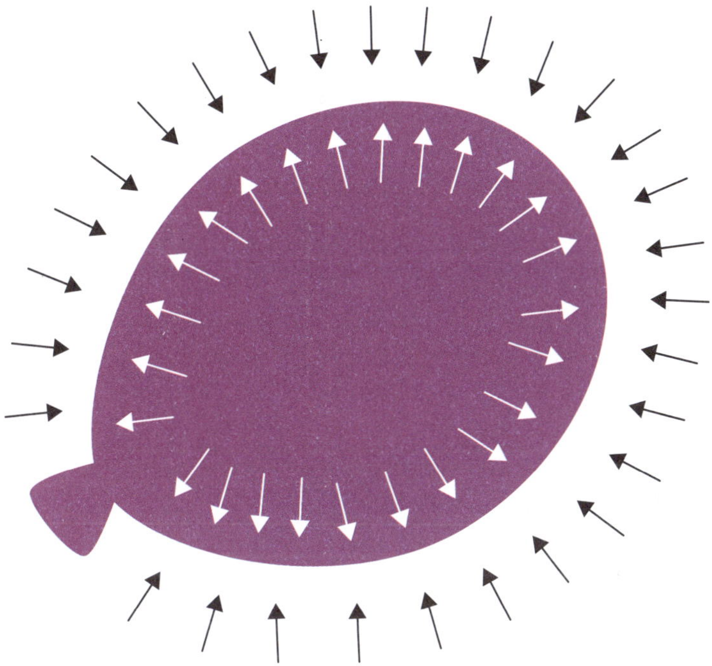

As a substance heats up, the atoms or molecules it is made of gain energy and move around more. If they are in an enclosed space, this increases the pressure. The air inside a balloon is already under pressure. Heating it has the same effect as putting even more air into it—that is, it creates more pressure, which is eventually too much for the rubber of the balloon.

35

Dinosaurs saw different stars

We think of the stars as being always the same, but they do change over very long periods of time. Millions of years ago, the stars looked very different.

For example, the group of stars called the Pleiades is just 100 million years old. That means they weren't even around when Stegosaurus was looking up at the sky.

New stars ...

Stars form from vast clouds of gas in space. A gas cloud is pulled in and forced together by its own gravity, squashing the gas closer and closer together. Eventually it's so compressed there is no room for the atoms to move. That's when nuclear fusion begins, and hydrogen atoms begin to fuse into helium atoms, releasing the energy that makes stars glow. All this takes a few million years, but it's happening all the time—there are always new stars being born somewhere.

... and old stars

As well as stars appearing in the sky, some stars disappear from it. When a star reaches the end of its life, it can either explode in a supernova or begin to fade away. If it fades, it becomes too dim to see without a telescope. Some stars that were once bright enough to see are now gone. Others have exploded. The dinosaurs probably saw stars you don't see and missed out on stars you can see.

On the move

Some stars still exist, but they aren't in the same place relative to other stars or Earth. The whole solar system is moving through space, and so are other stars. The sky slowly changes all the time.

36 Water stays in a bucket upside-down...

... as long as it's moving fast enough! If you fill a bucket with water and whirl it around quickly, the water stays in the bucket, even when the bucket is on its side or upside down.

If you stop the bucket at the top of its journey, the water will fall out. But if both water and bucket keep moving, the momentum keeps the water in the bucket.

Feel the force

Some people explain the water staying in the bucket as "centrifugal force," which means a force that makes things fly away from the middle of a circle when moving. But this force doesn't really exist. What actually happens is that the water "wants" to keep going in the same direction as it's already moving. This is a force called "inertia."

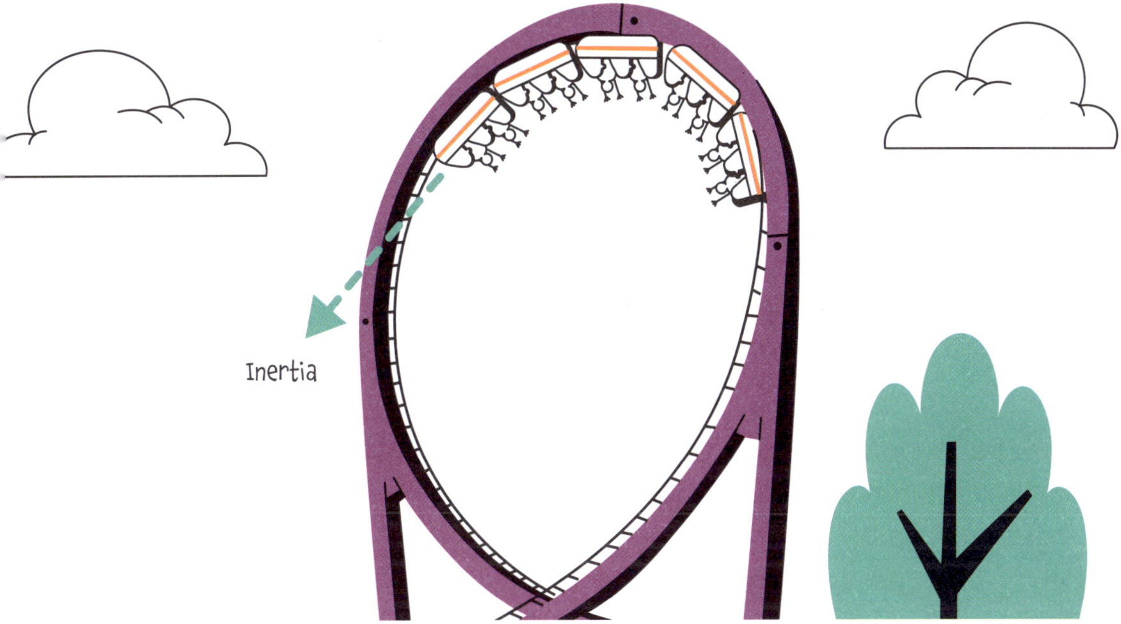

Keep going

At the start of the upswing, the water is going up. As the bucket comes to the top of the curve, the water is moving at an angle, but still up. The walls of the bucket keep it in so it doesn't go swooshing off into the sky. As the bucket starts to come down, the water would still like to keep going in a straight line—it doesn't want to go straight down. The bucket keeps it in (and you stay dry!)

The same thing keeps a roller coaster working. The cars have inertia, and would like to hurtle off into space, but the track prevents them doing so.

37 A feather and a hammer fall at the same speed

If you drop a feather and a hammer in a place with no air, they will both hit the ground at the same time.

You'd think that a heavier thing would fall faster than a light thing, but the speed at which an object falls is not affected by its weight (or mass). Gravity acts on all objects in the same way. The Italian scientist Galileo Galilei suggested an experiment 450 years ago that would prove it, and the experiment was finally carried out by astronaut David Scott in 1971. He dropped a feather and a metal hammer on the Moon, where there is no air, and they both fell at the same rate.

Shapely falling

If you drop a feather and a hammer at the same time on Earth, the hammer will reach the ground first. That's because air resistance, or "drag," keeps the feather from falling quickly. If you drop a flat sheet of paper and an identical sheet scrunched into a ball, the scrunched sheet will fall fastest, showing mass isn't the issue. Drag occurs because molecules in the air collide with the falling face of the object. An object with a larger surface facing in its direction of movement will experience more drag. That's because there's more space for collisions with air molecules.

DID YOU KNOW?

The feather Scott dropped was from a falcon—chosen because the lunar lander was named *Falcon*. The feather and the hammer are still on the Moon.

38 The Sun produces heat at the same rate as a compost heap

The Sun produces energy, including light and heat, by fusing hydrogen into helium. It converts about 600 million tons of hydrogen every second. If you had a block of the Sun's core that measured 1 m (3.3 ft) in each direction, it would produce only enough energy to run a fridge! Luckily, the Sun is very big.

Hot veg

In a compost heap, vegetation slowly rots away. The action of bacteria, fungi, and creatures like worms and insects breaks it down. The chemical reactions release heat. If you put your hand deep into an active compost heap (yuck, maybe don't), it would feel warm. But a compost heap is small, so the total energy produced isn't very great. A compost heap the size of the Sun would produce way more heat.

39 "Sunlight" can travel for thousands of years inside the Sun

The Sun releases energy as photons: tiny packets of light, heat, or other types of radiation. But to become the sunlight that streams out into space, they need to travel a long way.

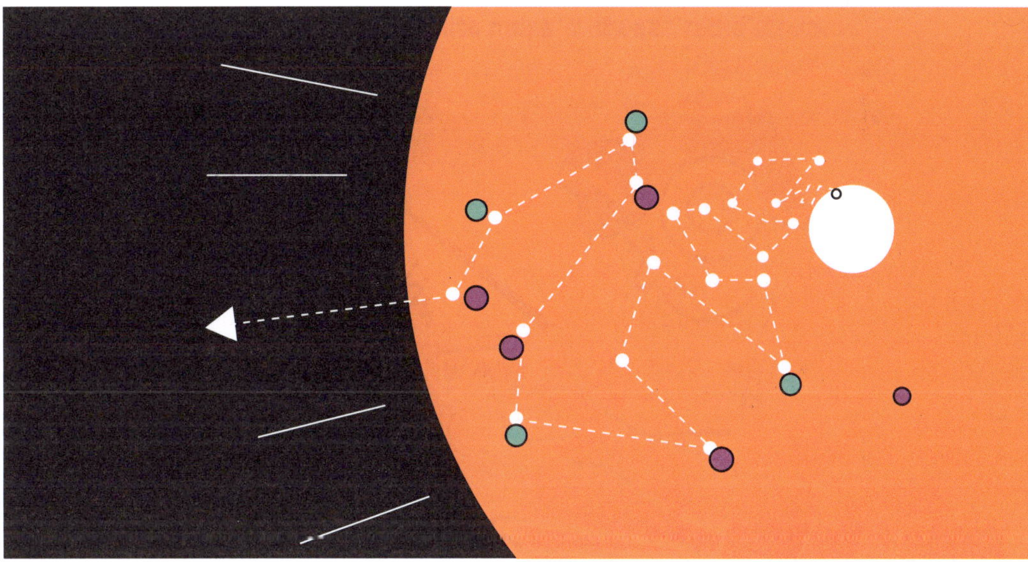

It's 695,700 km (432,300 mi) from the very middle of the Sun to the edge, but that's in a straight line. Photons don't go in a straight line because they're not trying to get out. They are jostled about randomly, absorbed, broken and recombined, and then head off in whichever direction a collision sends them. They only ever reach the edge of the Sun by chance. Then they can escape into space. The journey can take anything from a few seconds to more than a million years.

40 The Sun Is just 20 (galactic) years old

You have a birthday every year—one for each time the Earth goes around the Sun. But when is the Sun's birthday? While Earth goes around the Sun, the Sun goes around the middle of our galaxy, the Milky Way. Indeed, the whole galaxy spins around.

The Sun, Earth, our Moon, and all the other planets, moons, asteroids, and comets are turning around in space as a group, along with all the others stars in the galaxy. The solar system takes 230 million years to make a complete circuit around the mid-point of the Milky Way. As the solar system is 4.6 billion (4,600 million) years old, that means it's made 20 circuits since the solar system formed—it's 20 galactic years old.

Wish you were here?

The last time Earth was in its current place in the galaxy was 230 million years ago, when the dinosaurs were only just getting started.

Using the "galactic year" to measure time, the dinosaurs disappeared only a third of a year ago, the Milky Way itself formed 54 years ago, and the Big Bang was around 60 years ago.

41 We're heading for a smash!

The Milky Way isn't standing still. Even as our solar system orbits the middle of the Milky Way, the galaxy itself is hurtling through space at about 2 million km (1.2 million mi) per hour. In around 4 billion years' time, it will collide with the next nearest galaxy, Andromeda. It won't be as disastrous as it sounds, as both galaxies are mostly empty space and will probably merge peacefully.

42 Stones can jump!

They need a helping hand, but if you throw a stone at just the right angle you can get it to "skip" over water, bouncing and jumping a few times before it sinks.

Speed and spin

Spin and speed keep a stone skipping. You have to throw the stone parallel to the water surface so that it stays flat and spins in the air. The spin keeps it moving, with its trailing edge near the water rather than tipping over, and makes it stable in air. The faster the spin, the more it will skip. Spinning five times per second, it will skip five times.

The best skipping stones are flat, and heavy enough not to be blown off course by the wind.

DID YOU KNOW?

The record for stone skipping is 88 bounces, achieved by Kurt Steiner in 2013.

Waterskiing for stones

Stones skip by dragging the back (trailing) edge across the water, pushing up a little "pile" of water in front. The stone then rides up the watery slope and launches into the air. Gravity soon pulls it down, where it strikes the surface and does the same thing again. It's rather like water-skiing, which pushes water in front of the ski and the ski then rides up. With each skip, gravity pulls the stone farther into the water and the water then produces more drag on the stone. Eventually, it can't escape any more and sinks.

DID YOU KNOW?

During the Second World War, Britain used "bouncing bombs" to destroy German dams from a distance. The idea was based on skipping stones.

43 There's enough sunlight every hour to power everything on Earth for a year

In theory, everything on Earth could easily be solar powered, and we could give up on fossil fuels such as coal, oil, and gas forever. Energy from the Sun needs to be converted to electricity to be useful, but luckily that's quite easy to do.

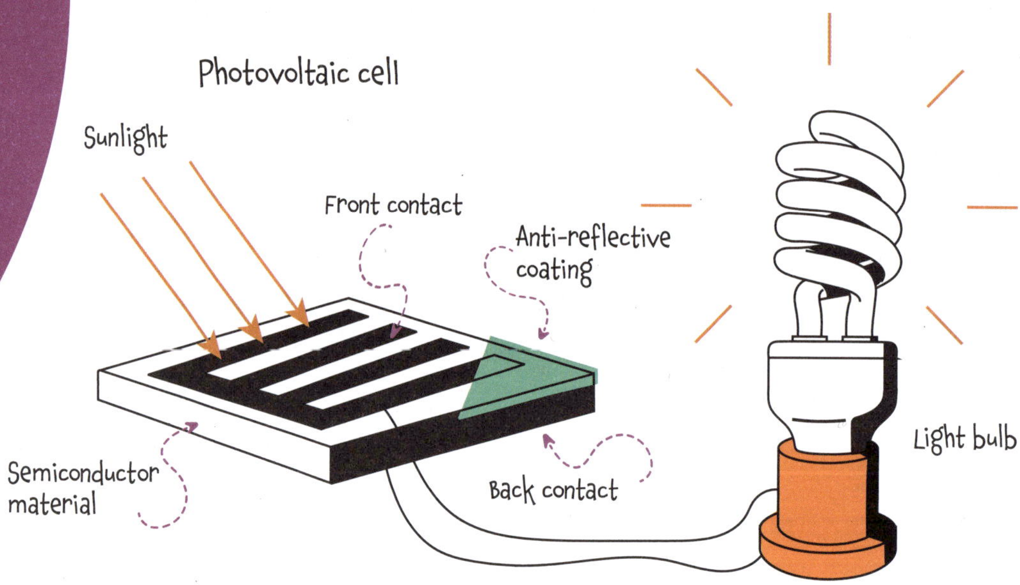

Trapping sunlight

A solar cell, or photovoltaic cell, converts the energy of sunlight into useful electrical energy. It does this by using the photons in sunlight to knock electrons out of a special type of material called a semiconductor and get them to flow in one direction. A flow of electrons makes an electric current.

The electrons move to the front of the photovoltaic cell, so the front has a negative charge, and the back, with fewer electrons, has a positive charge. If the front and back are connected by a wire, a current flows through the wire. It can be used to light a bulb, or more usefully, carry electricity away to be used elsewhere or stored in a battery.

Making light work

Each photovoltaic cell is small, but they're used in groups—from the little module that might recharge a phone, right up to the panels you might have on a roof and the huge arrays in a solar energy farm.

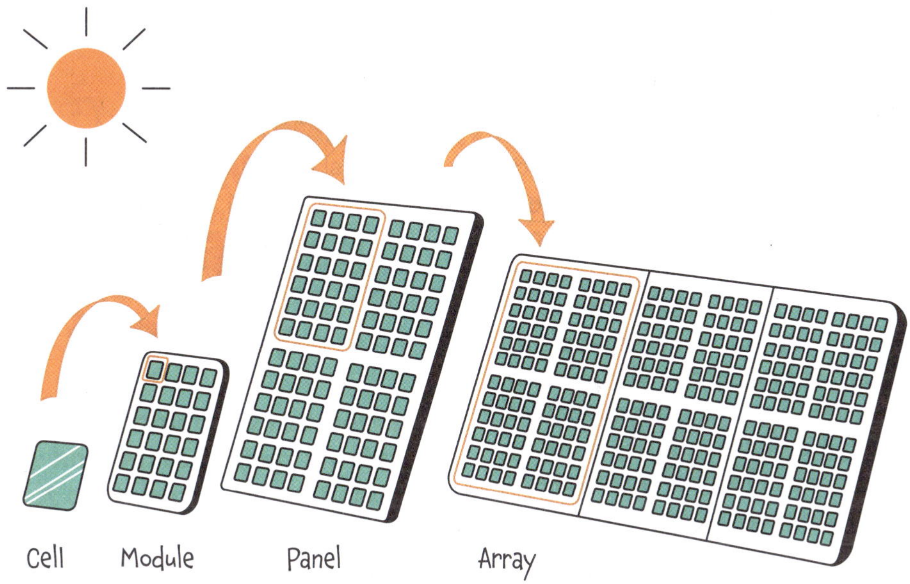

DID YOU KNOW?

Reptiles are solar powered! They need heat from sunlight to warm up and do their reptile-y thing. (Though they do also need food.) That's why you see lizards basking in the sun.

44 A black hole would turn you into spaghetti

Going into a black hole wouldn't change you into pasta, but it would pull your body out of shape so that you would look like a long string of spaghetti!

No hole here

A black hole sounds like it should be something with nothing in it—that's what a hole usually is. But a black hole is actually a place with too much in it. It's somewhere that matter is so squashed that it's incredibly dense, with lots of mass forced into a very small space. Gravity makes objects with mass move in the direction of each other; those with the most mass have the most gravitational "pull." A black hole exerts so much gravity that not even light can escape—and that's why it's black.

Pulled in

If you got too close to a black hole its gravity would drag you to it. When you got closer still, the gravity would exert such a strong pull on you that it would be different even over the length of your body. If you were approaching feet-first, the effect of gravity would be greater on your feet than on your head, so your feet would be pulled in more quickly than your head. And the result of that would be that your feet went faster and faster into the black hole while your head couldn't catch up. You would be stretched into a spaghetti shape and eventually pulled apart entirely. So stay away from black holes!

45 You can't swim in honey

But neither will you drown if you fall in a vast vat of honey. Honey is denser than the human body, so you'll float. As long as you make sure you're upright, you can stay there until rescued—you won't sink.

Through thick and thin

Honey is a viscous liquid, which means it's thick and flows very slowly. Some honey is so thick it seems solid, and you have to scoop it out with a knife or spoon. Other honey is quite runny—you can pour it, but it still doesn't flow like water. Viscosity is a measure of how resistant a liquid is to flowing. Water is not at all viscous; it will run all over the place if you spill it.

A liquid is viscous if there are forces between its molecules that tend to hold them together, so layers won't slide over each other. Water has only small forces between the molecules and so when you walk or swim through water, you can easily push it aside. Honey has stronger forces, so it's much harder to push it aside. If it's too hard, and your muscles aren't strong enough to push through, it will stick to you, causing massive drag (see page 65).

Warm it up!

You might have more luck escaping from honey if it's warm. The viscosity reduces as the temperature increases. This also means that if your runny honey has hardened, you can put it in the microwave to make it more spreadable, even if you aren't going to swim in it.

46 Some trains float in the air

It sounds like sci-fi, but there are trains that don't touch their tracks. "Maglev" trains float just above the track because they are held up and moved along by magnets. Maglev means "magnetic levitation."

Magnets on and off

Magnets can do more than stick to your fridge. Powerful magnets can lift and move heavy objects, including trains. These are electromagnets. Unlike a fridge magnet, an electromagnet isn't permanently magnetic. Electromagnets are produced when an electric current flows through a wire. When the power is turned off, it stops being magnetic. The magnetic field created by the current is at right angles to the direction of flow of the current.

North and south

Magnets have a north pole and a south pole. Opposite poles are attracted to each other, so a north and south pole will pull to each other. Like poles repel each other, so two north poles will push apart. Maglev trains work using a combination of attraction and repulsion.

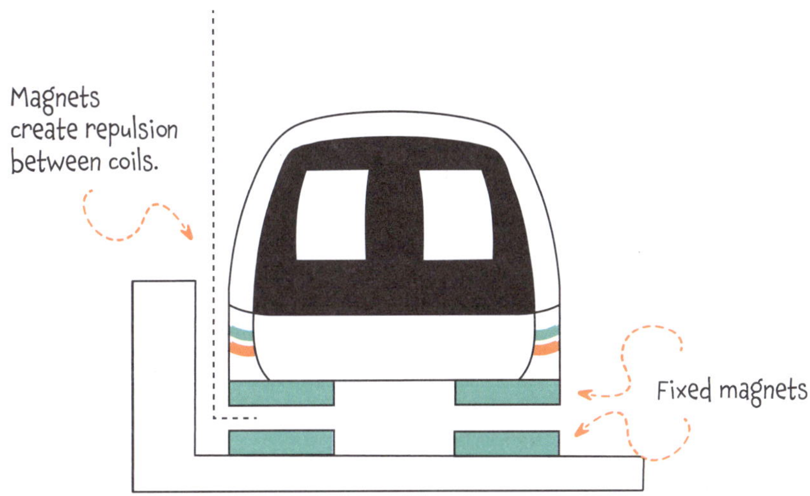

Pushing and pulling

There are different types of Maglev trains. In an "Inductrack" Maglev train system, powerful magnets line the underside of the train and metal coils line the guideway. An electric current passes through the coils to create a magnetic field. The train is kept floating above the guideway by magnetic repulsion between the coils and the fixed magnets.

More magnets and coils line the side of the train and guideway. Switching the direction of the current changes the magnetic field to pull and push the train forward. The train is not slowed by friction, and it doesn't bump and shake like trains that have wheels running on tracks. It's quieter, faster, and more comfortable than a regular train.

47 If ice didn't float on water, we wouldn't be here

Unlike most substances, water is less dense as a solid than a liquid. That's why ice floats to the top of a drink of water and icebergs stick up out of the sea. Water is at its most dense at 4°C (40°F)—surprising!

Under an icy blanket

If ice sank, a freezing river, lake, or sea would freeze from the bottom. Instead, water at 4°C sinks to the bottom and a layer of ice forms above. That layer insulates the water below from the cold air, preventing it from freezing. Liquid water below the ice gives fish and other organisms somewhere to survive. In Earth's distant past, there have been very cold periods, called Snowball Earth episodes, when Earth's whole surface has frozen. Luckily, water beneath the icy crust stayed warm enough for organisms to survive until conditions improved.

Insulator or conductor?

An insulator slows or stops the movement of heat energy. You use an insulating material when you put on a warm coat or gloves. Fabric is an insulator. It also traps a layer of air near your body, and air is also a good insulator. Conductors of heat allow heat to travel through them. Metals are conductors. They feel cold to the touch, even at room temperature, because they quickly conduct heat away from your body. You can tell whether something is likely to be an insulator or conductor of heat by whether it feels warm (like fabric) or cold (like metal) at room temperature.

48 The sky on Venus is orange

While sky on Earth looks blue, it looks different elsewhere. On Venus, it's a mix of orange and yellow. On Mars, it's pink.

Looking up

For a planet to have "sky" it needs an atmosphere, which is a layer of gas surrounding the planet. Without an atmosphere, looking up you would just see the black of space, with stars or the Sun shining. This is how the sky looks from the Moon and from Mercury.

Sky blue, sky ... yellow?

Sunlight looks white, but it is made up of a whole spectrum, from red to violet (see page 36). Light travels as waves of energy, with red having the longest wavelength and blue and violet the shortest wavelength. Earth's atmosphere is made mostly of nitrogen and oxygen, which both have small molecules. Light with a longer wavelength is not much disrupted by these molecules. But blue light, with its short wavelength, is bounced around all over the place. This is called scattering, and it's why the sky looks blue on Earth.

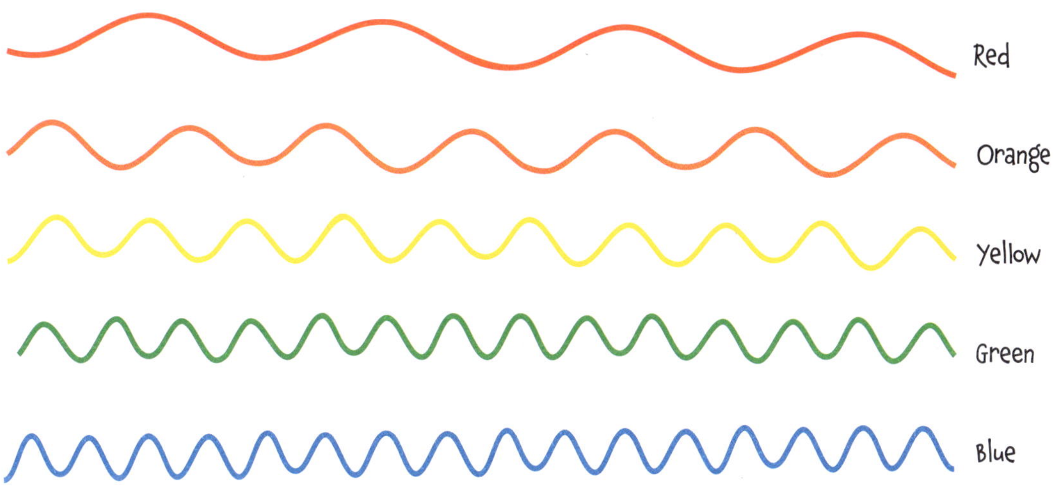

On Venus, the atmosphere is mostly carbon dioxide, but it has a lot of thick clouds of sulfuric acid. Mars has a thin atmosphere, but it contains a lot of dust. Clouds and dust scatter light differently from gases as the particles are larger. They affect light with a shorter wavelength more. On Venus they scatter light in the orange and yellow areas of the spectrum most, making the sky look orange overall. On Mars, the sky looks pinkish-red by day, but sunsets are blue!

49 A plane can go so fast that it overtakes its own sound

If you hear a loud boom from a plane flying overhead, don't assume it's going to crash—it's just going faster than the speed of the sound! A supersonic (faster than sound) plane makes a noise called a sonic boom when it reaches the speed of sound, which is 343 m (1,125 ft) per second, or 1,234 km (767 mi) per hour.

Spreading sound

Pressure waves spread out in the air in front of and behind the moving plane, like water waves spreading out in front of and behind a boat. As the plane goes faster, the waves in front of it get closer together until eventually they can't get out of the way fast enough and crash into each other. That releases energy as sound. It sounds like a thunderclap or a cannon firing.

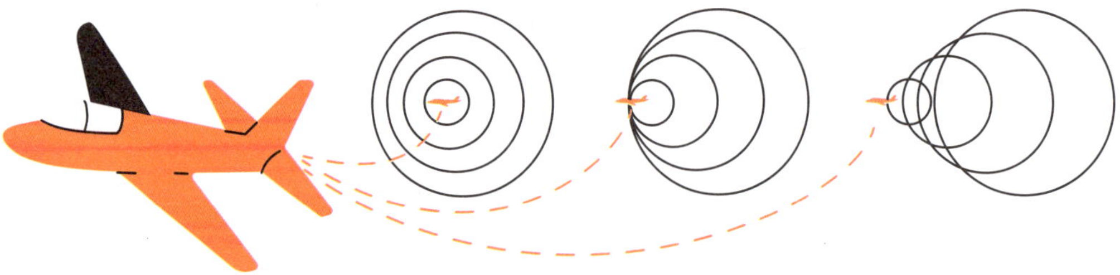

Wave after wave

Although someone on the ground will hear one loud boom as a plane passes, the colliding pressure waves happen constantly while the plane flies at a supersonic speed. You only hear it when you are in just the right place, but elsewhere people hear it at other times. Because the plane goes faster than sound, you can see it overhead before you hear the noise of the boom.

DID YOU KNOW?

When the ringmaster in a circus cracks a whip, the tip of the whip moves faster than the speed of sound —that's why it makes a noise.

50 Most of the Universe is a complete mystery

The normal matter that makes up all the things around you, including your body, accounts for only around four percent of the Universe. The remaining 96 percent is known as "dark matter" and "dark energy," which scientists know very little about.

Spinning too fast

Scientists can work out the mass of a galaxy from how fast it spins. But when they started looking at galaxies, they found the calculated mass was about five times higher than it should be for what we know is there. They called the missing matter "dark matter" because we can't see it (only the darkness of space itself is visible). With dark matter, something is there, but no one knows exactly what "it" is. Some of it could be objects that don't produce or reflect light—like failed stars that never grew big enough to glow, burned-out stars, or black holes. But there's too much dark matter for it all to be things like this. It might be something we haven't discovered yet.

Pushing apart

As if that wasn't strange enough, it turns out there's also some strange energy that makes up even more of the Universe. All the normal matter and dark matter only make up around 28 percent of the total Universe—there's another 72 percent of something else. Scientists call it "dark energy," which they think is a force that pushes galaxies further apart, making the Universe expand (grow bigger). That's right! The Universe is continually expanding outward!

51 Balloons make your hair stand on end

If you rub a balloon against a wool or acrylic sweater and then hold it near your head, the balloon will attract your hair to it. This is because static electricity has built up on the surface of the balloon.

Historic demo

Scientist Stephen Gray demonstrated static electricity in 1729. He suspended a boy from silk ropes and charged him with static electricity, then showed how shreds of paper and ash would jump up to the boy's skin. (This didn't harm the boy.)

Electricity without batteries

You're probably familiar with static electricity already. If you've ever got a tiny electric prickle from touching metal, or tried the hair trick with a balloon, you've already met it.

Static electricity is created when surfaces rub together and electrons are ripped from one surface and build up on another. The surface with extra electrons then has a negative charge, as every electron carries a tiny negative electrical charge. If a balloon has built up static electricity on its surface, it will attract your hair, which has less negative charge, pulling it to the balloon.

Conductors and insulators

Materials that conduct electricity allow electrons to move easily through them. Insulators don't allow electricity to move. The silk ropes in Gray's experiment were insulators, so none of the electricity escaped from the boy through them. Conductors can be linked together to carry electricity over a long distance, whether that's static electricity or the mains electricity you use in your home.

52 The Moon is trying to get away!

It's not going to up and run off one day, but it's slowly sneaking off into space.

The Moon formed 4.5 billion years ago when a planet the size of Mars crashed into Earth. It was a mighty mess, but as things settled down, all the smashed-up bits collected together to form the Moon. The Moon formed very near Earth, just 24,000–32,000 km (15,000–20,000 mi) away. That might sound like a long way off, but it's only the same distance as a round trip from New York to Singapore.

Today, the Moon is 386,000 km (240,00 mi) away—more than 10–15 times as far. Its escape started with a mad dash, covering the first 110,000 km (68,000 mi) in just 500 million years, so 22 cm (8.5 in) a year. It's slowed down, and is now creeping away at 3.8 cm (1.5 in) each year. If you live to be 90, the Moon will be 3.4 m (11 ft) farther away than it was when you were born.

53 The Moon looked slightly bigger to the dinosaurs

The Moon was a bit closer to Earth when the dinosaurs were around. If there had been any people here to see the Moon in the sky (there weren't), it would have appeared as a huge red ball of glowing hot lava (molten rock)—kind of like a volcano that has erupted.

You can make a spring "walk" on its own

A Slinky is a special type of spring, sold as a toy, that will walk down a flight of stairs—but it won't walk over a flat surface. A Slinky uses the potential, or stored, energy it has when it's not moving at the top of a staircase and converts it into kinetic, or movement, energy as you start it walking down the stairs. The momentum of the kinetic energy keeps it going!

Don't stop!

Momentum is a force produced by mass and speed. It's what keeps something moving once it has started to move. A heavy object moving at speed will keep moving until something stops it. On Earth, objects are eventually stopped by air resistance or friction with the ground if they don't meet another obstacle. This is the reason people need to wear a seatbelt in a car. If the car stops suddenly (or crashes), the momentum is enough to keep any lose objects (and people) in the car moving. Without a seatbelt, passengers will continue to move—and likely get hurt—as they hit the inside of the car.

A Slinky keeps going downstairs for the same reason. It has enough momentum to flip over when it has gathered on one step, and so it keeps falling down the next step. Gravity keeps pulling it down, but it needs the kick of movement to start each step. When it gets to flat ground it stops—there's nowhere else to go! But it will "walk" along a sloping board or down a hill, because again gravity helps it along.

55 The Sun is green

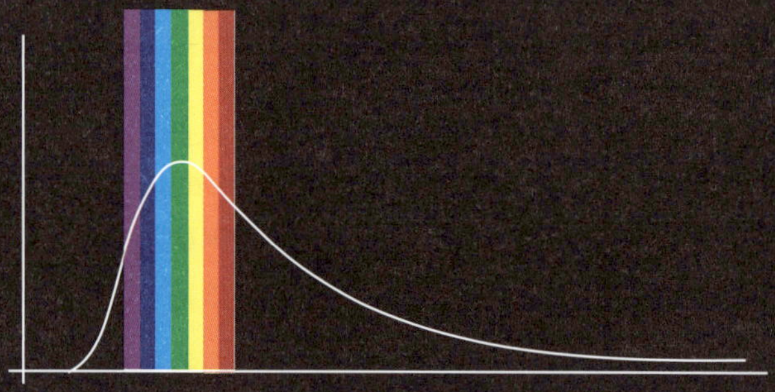

You should never look directly at the Sun, but we've all seen enough of it to know it doesn't look green. The Sun sends out light across the spectrum that looks white, but it actually sends out a bit more green light than anything else.

Star light, star white

In the night sky the stars all look white, but astronomers can identify some as red and others as yellow, orange, or blue. How they look depends on which is their peak wavelength—the wavelength of the light they emit most—and that depends on how hot they are. The coolest stars are red; a bit hotter and they look orange. The very hottest stars are blue.

In the eye of the beholder

The Sun sends out light of all colors, and, although green is the most common, we will never see the light as green due to the way our eyes work. Our eyes mix all the light together to make white. The Sun would have to put out only green light for it to look green to us.

56

One day, the Sun will swallow Earth ...

But not for billions of years from now. The Sun is too small to end in a supernova. Instead, it will swell up, growing so large it will engulf Mercury, Venus, and Earth. Earth's oceans will boil away and anything living will burn up.

Dying light

The Sun will be much bigger, but also cooler. As it runs out of its hydrogen fuel, it will glow red instead of white, and will finally become so cold that it doesn't glow at all—it will be a dark lump turning coldly in space.

57 We can't predict the weather

It seems that whenever you depend on the weather forecast to plan a day out, it turns out to be wrong. This isn't too surprising: predicting the weather is incredibly complex, and we can't make an accurate prediction more than a few days in advance.

Chaos reigns

Weather is an example of something scientists call a "chaotic" system. Normally, we think of chaos as being completely disordered. Your room becomes chaotic if you never put anything away, and the result is you can't find whatever you're looking for. But to scientists, "chaotic" doesn't mean completely disordered. Instead, it means a very complex system in which there are so many variables (things that can change) that it's virtually impossible to take account of all the possible things that could happen to make a reliable prediction.

Butterflies and storms

The chaotic nature of the weather system is sometimes explained by people saying a butterfly flapping its wings can cause a storm the other side of the world. It doesn't mean storms are literally caused by butterflies; just that small changes can have a massive effect. The so-called "butterfly effect" was discovered by mathematician Edward Lorenz when he ran a weather prediction he had made a second time and got a completely different result. He'd used the same data, but instead of using exactly the same numbers with all their decimal places, he'd entered the numbers to only two decimal places (so accurate to only one hundredth). These tiny changes were enough to change the weather prediction entirely.

58 Footprints on the Moon are there forever

The twelve astronauts who have been to the Moon have left their footprints (and a lot of trash and equipment) behind. These will stay there for a very long time, as the Moon has neither wind to blow dust over them nor internal movement that can change its surface.

Wind and weather

On Earth, footprints in dust, sand, or dry soil are quickly lost. Either more material settles over them, carried by the wind, or the material they have been left in blows away. If it rains, they can be lost more quickly. But on the Moon, there is no wind or weather.

The moon is a quiet place

Earth is also a very active place. The continents move around all the time, and new rock is added to Earth's surface in volcanic eruptions. Rock is constantly recycled over hundreds of millions of years. This is driven by molten rock inside Earth, called magma, moving around and bursting out. The Moon doesn't have this internal activity. It's quiet, cold, and dead. No volcanoes will pour new rock over the footprints and left-behind Moon buggies. This is why the Moon is covered in craters but Earth is not. Earth has been hit by as many asteroids and meteors, but its scars have been covered.

Lost in space

The only way our relics on the Moon could be destroyed is if an asteroid crashes into the Moon's surface near where they are, destroying them or covering them with dust or rock. Otherwise, they'll be there for millions of years.

59 You have more energy after climbing a hill

When you climb a hill, you feel your muscles working and your body generating heat. It's an action that feels like it takes a lot energy. This type of energy is called "potential energy."

All types of energy

Energy is described by scientists as the ability to do work. There are different types of energy. A car uses the chemical energy freed by burning fuel, or the electric energy provided by a battery, to move it along. It converts the chemical or electrical energy into kinetic (movement) energy. Some energy is lost as heat—because no system is completely efficient.

Potential energy represents the possibility of doing something. A compressed spring has potential energy, and an arrow pulled back in a bow ready to fire at a target has potential energy. When the arrow is released, the potential energy is converted into movement, carrying the arrow forward. Once you have climbed a hill, you have the potential to roll down it!

Cycling uses less energy than walking

It might feel like you work harder to cycle than to walk, especially if you are going up a hill. But a bicycle is a very efficient machine. Little of the energy provided by your muscles is wasted and almost all is converted into movement.

If you cycle for an hour, you'll use more energy than if you walk for an hour—but you'll go much farther. If you compare going a mile by bike or on foot, you use less energy on a bike.

61 The first hovercraft was made from tin cans and a vacuum cleaner

The inventor of the hovercraft, Christopher Cockerell, tried out his idea by making a prototype—a working model—from an old coffee tin, a cat food tin, weighing scales, and a hair dryer.

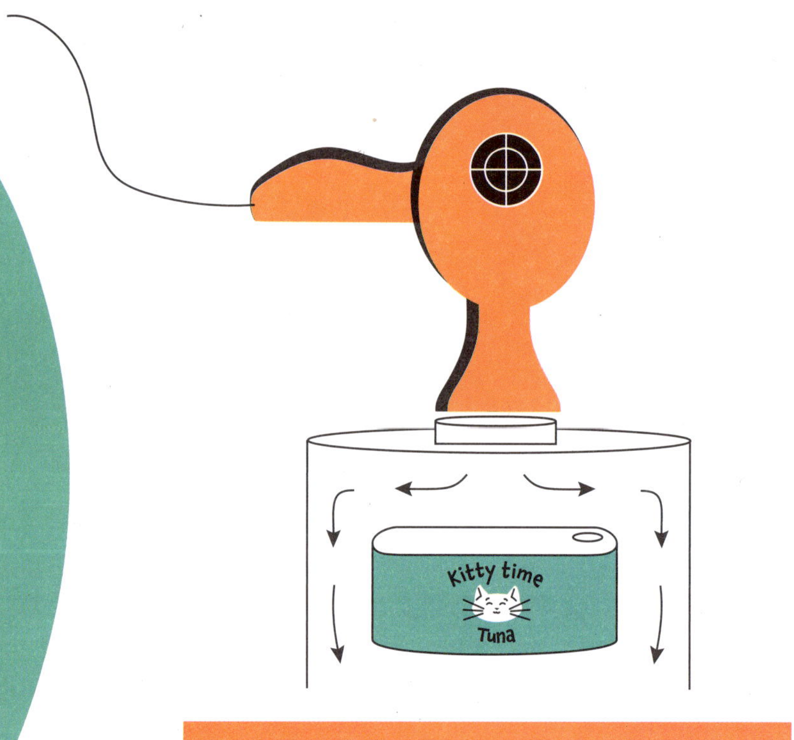

Walking on air

A hovercraft works by using fans driven by an engine to create a cushion of air underneath the craft, pushing it up off the surface of the sea. A different set of fans, used like the propellers of a plane, drive the craft over waves or even over land.

It's not a drag

A hovercraft is a very efficient way of moving over water because there is little drag. Drag is the effect of water (or air) slowing down a craft moving through it. It affects boats, planes, and even cars. Vehicles that move through water or air are generally a streamlined shape so that the water or air flows over them easily. Hovercraft don't experience drag from water—the craft floats above, rather than moves through, the sea.

How it works

Giant blowers produce air that enters the chamber of the hovercraft. Rubber "skirts" on the bottom trap most of the air underneath the craft, creating a balloonlike effect, which allows it to float above waves and on land surfaces.

62 The horizon is closer on the Moon than on Earth

If you stand on a beach or in an open field, you can see all the way to the horizon. On a clear day, that's about 5 km (3 mi). But on the Moon, the horizon is closer at about 2.4 km (1.5 mi). Because the Moon is smaller than Earth, it curves away from you more quickly.

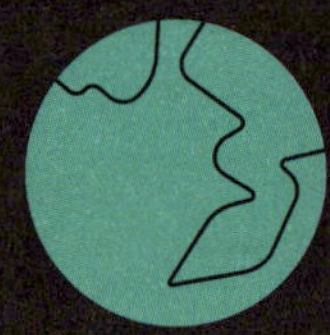

See farther from a hill

If you stand on a hill, you can see farther. If you stood at the top of Mount Everest, you could see 370 km (230 mi). This difference is how even the ancient Greeks knew that Earth is not flat. If it were, you wouldn't be able to see farther by going higher. You can also see things that stick up above the horizon even when you can't see their base.

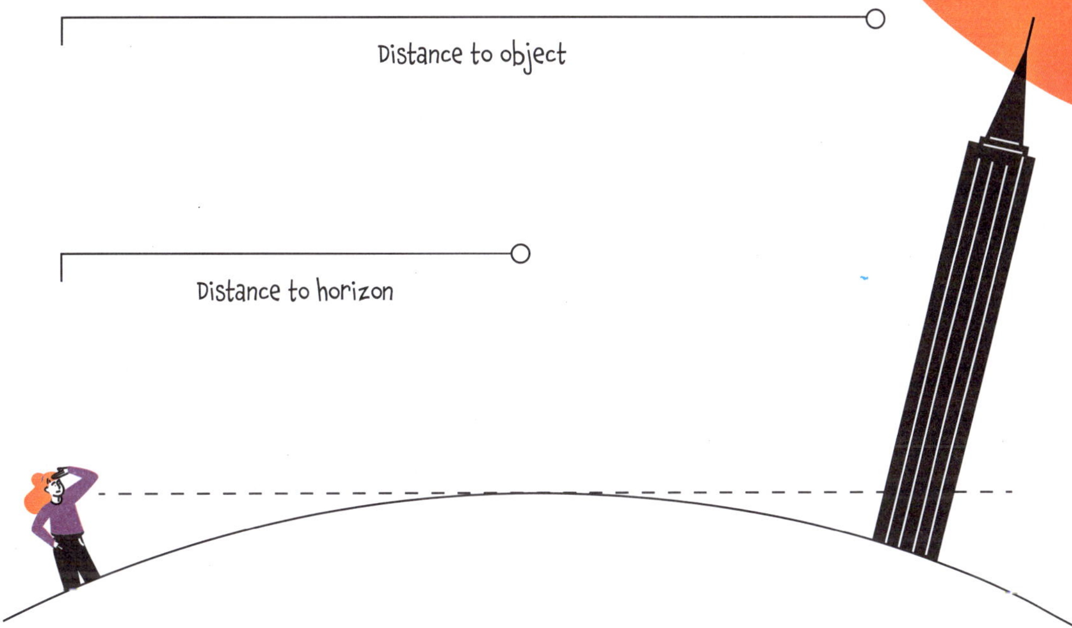

You can see the sunset twice in one day

If you watch the sunset from low down—on a beach, say—and then run to a high place, you might be in time to see it set again. That's because as you see farther round the world from up high, you can see the Sun when it's lower in the sky. In fact, the Sun isn't moving; it's that Earth is turning away from the Sun.

63 Earth is wonky

Earth doesn't stand up straight in space—it leans at an angle. The only reason we have summer and winter in the north and south hemispheres is because of its wonkiness.

All around the world

Earth makes one complete turn on its axis each day, and that's what makes a day. At the same time, Earth is orbiting (going around) the Sun. It takes a year for Earth to make one circuit around the Sun.

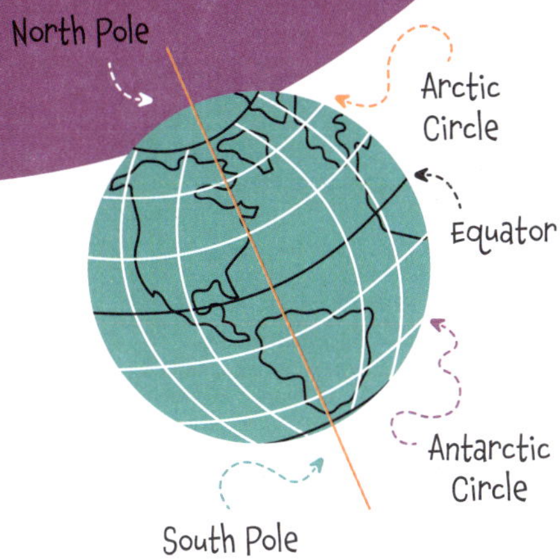

Tipped over

Earth rotates around an imaginary line (axis) between the North Pole and the South Pole. But that axis is tilted in space when compared with the path Earth takes around the Sun. As it orbits the Sun, the top and bottom—the Northern and Southern Hemispheres—are tilted toward or away from the Sun. When your part of Earth is tilted toward the Sun, it's summer and the days are longer. When your part is tilted away from the Sun, it's winter and the days are shorter. At the equator (an imaginary line around the middle of the Earth), days and nights are about the same length year round, and there are no clear summer and winter seasons.

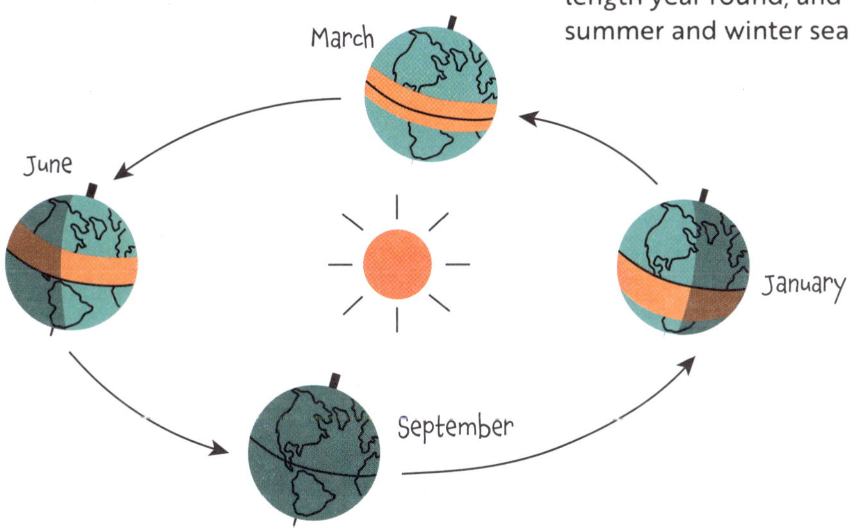

Knocked off balance

When Earth was formed, it was upright, with a line between the North Pole and the South Poles being at right angles to Earth's path around the Sun. But a massive collision early in its history knocked it over, creating the Moon at the same time (see page 90).

64 You couldn't fall through Earth, even if a hole went all the way through

Humans haven't managed to drill all the way through Earth's top layer, called the crust, let alone all the way through. Even if we could make a hole straight through Earth, you'd stop in the middle if you fell into the hole.

The middle is where it's at

Gravity pulls things to the middle of Earth, which is the central point of Earth's mass. If a hole went through Earth, you would fall to the middle, but there would be no force to pull you through to the other side, so you would just stop there. The force of gravity right at the middle of Earth would also be so powerful that you couldn't climb back out either.

65

Earth isn't a perfect sphere

But nor is it flat! Earth is a slightly squashed sphere, called an "oblate spheroid." It's fatter in the middle (around the equator) than if measured pole to pole. If you stand at the equator, you're 21.4 km (13.3 mi) farther from the middle of Earth than you would be standing at one of the poles.

Earth as a pizza

Have you ever seen someone making a pizza base from pizza dough? As they spin it around, the momentum causes the lump of dough to flatten. Earth is a lot firmer than a blob of pizza dough, and subject to far more gravitational "pull" (see page 123)—that's why Earth isn't pizza shaped.

66 You can break glass by singing

Sound can break glass if it's loud enough and at the right frequency. Opera singers, who are trained to sing loudly, can break a glass by singing at it. The frequency of their voice makes the glass vibrate. As the sound grows louder, the glass vibrates more, until eventually it breaks. (Don't try this at home!)

Frequency

The frequency of a sound is what we hear as its pitch—how high or low it is. Squeaking is a high-pitched sound, with a high frequency. Rumbling thunder is a low-pitched sound, with a low frequency. Frequency is measured in Hertz.

Loud and soft

The volume of a sound is measured in decibels. A normal conversation is held at about 50 decibels. A loud lawnmower runs at about 100 decibels. Around 100 decibels is the volume needed to break glass. Luckily, window glass is held in frames which "damps" it, stilling the vibrations, so the windows don't break when someone mows the lawn!

It resonates

Glass has a natural resonance. This is a frequency at which it will start to vibrate. Different glasses resonate at slightly different frequencies, depending on their shape and structure. If you gently flick the edge of a glass, it will make a "ping" sound at its resonant frequency. With sound of just that frequency, the glass will vibrate a great deal. Increasing the volume of the noise will eventually shatter the glass.

67 Sunlight can push a spacecraft along

Tiny spacecraft fitted with "solar sails" can be driven through space by photons—tiny parcels of light energy coming from the Sun.

Giving a push

Photons don't have any mass, but they do have momentum, produced by their movement. If a photon hits a solar sail, it passes its momentum to the sail, which drives the spacecraft forward a little. As there are lots of photons, all the tiny bits of momentum add up to a good push.

No resistance

There's no resistance to movement in space. On Earth, drag from the air or friction with the ground slows down anything moving, but in space movement continues unhindered. As more and more photons hit the sail, the spacecraft goes faster and faster.

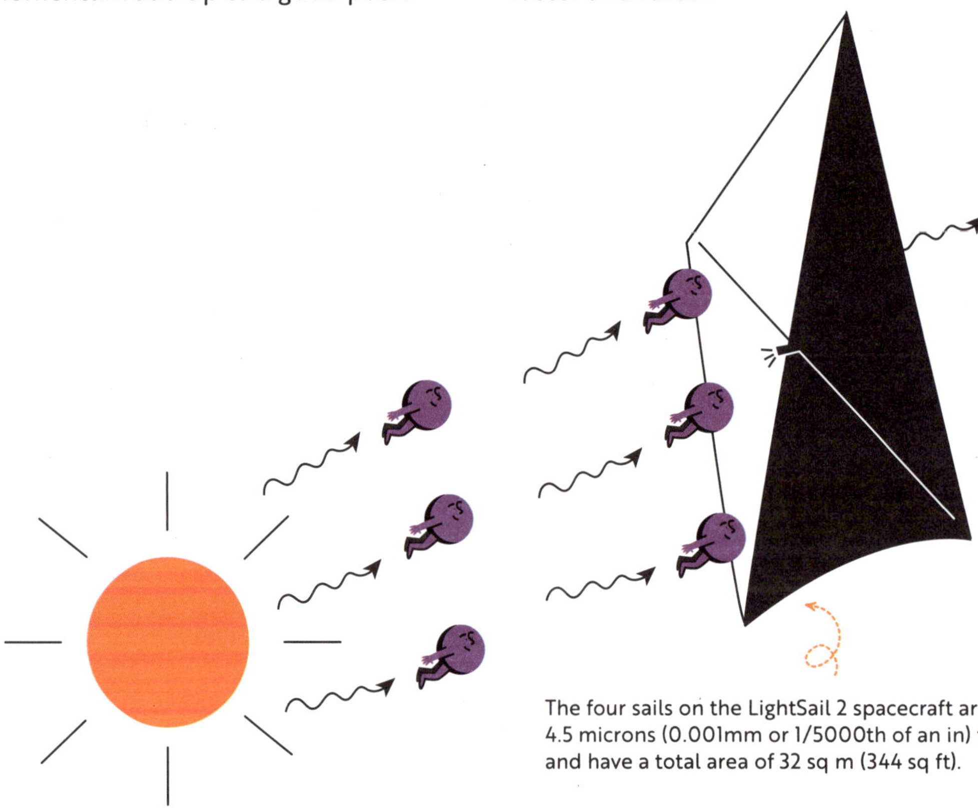

The four sails on the LightSail 2 spacecraft are just 4.5 microns (0.001mm or 1/5000th of an in) thick and have a total area of 32 sq m (344 sq ft).

68 You weigh more in sunlight than in shade

When you stand in sunlight, more photons from the Sun hit your body than if you stand in the shade or in darkness. Photons can't add mass to you, but their momentum pushes you against Earth, adding to your weight. Weight is the effect of gravity on mass. Although your mass doesn't increase, the effect of gravity is increased by the push from the photons.

Heavy city

It's been calculated that the city of Chicago—which weighs quite a lot anyway—weighs 140 kg (300 lb) more on a sunny day than on a cloudy day. That's the effect of all the extra photons pushing down on it!

69 The Universe used to be orange or red

If you look at the night sky, you'll see it's mostly black with a few spots of light where there are stars and planets. But if you'd been able to see it 13.7 billion years ago, it would have been orange.

First light

The Universe started with the "Big Bang," nearly 13.8 billion years ago. Matter and energy burst into being from nowhere. At first there was nothing to see (and nothing to see the nothing), but after 378,000 years, conditions in the Universe had changed enough for hydrogen nuclei (the middles of hydrogen atoms) to trap electrons and become hydrogen atoms. As the atoms stabilized, they released photons—tiny packets of light—that streamed through the Universe. Energy in the form of photons has a wavelength, which is the distance between the peak of one wave of energy and the peak of the next wave. The wavelength of this burst of light tells scientists it was probably orange or red, so the background of space would have been orange, not black.

Slowing down

Although the photons released near the start of the Universe are still around, they've stretched. You couldn't keep going at top speed for long, and after a few billion years, even photons are running out of energy. They don't slow down, but they do pack fewer up-and-down waves into the same distance. The result is that instead of waves of light, the left-over radiation is now radio waves. We can find it using radio telescopes, and you can even hear it in the "white noise" between radio stations.

70 An iron ball will take an hour to reach the seabed

If you dropped a heavy iron ball over the deepest part of the ocean, it would fall for an hour before settling. Yet if you dropped it the same distance through air, it would hit the ground in seconds. Not only is water denser than air, it gets even denser the deeper you go in the sea.

Dropping the soap

If you've ever dropped the soap in the bath or an object in a swimming pool, you'll have noticed that it falls more slowly than it does in air. Air is a gas, and the molecules in it are much farther apart than the molecules in water. At room temperature and pressure, most things you might drop in the air will fall almost as quickly as if you dropped it in a vacuum (a space that has been emptied of everything, including air). But in water, there are a lot more molecules in the same volume. They get in the way of something falling and slow it down.

Under pressure

In the deepest parts of the sea, the pressure produced by water from above pressing down is great. Molecules are packed closely together. This means anything you drop struggles to get through them to reach the seabed. A heavy lump sinking squashes the water beneath it, which helps to hold the lump up for longer.

71 The Sun is losing weight

Well, it's losing mass. The Sun produces light by fusing hydrogen at its core to make another gas, helium. But each helium atom has a little bit less mass than the hydrogen atoms it's made from—so the Sun gets lighter and lighter.

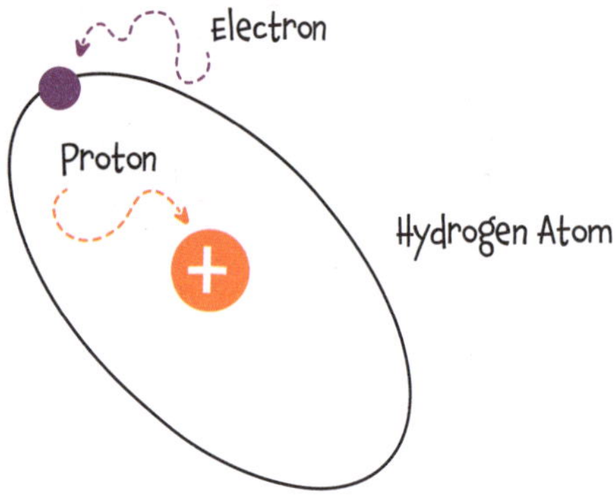

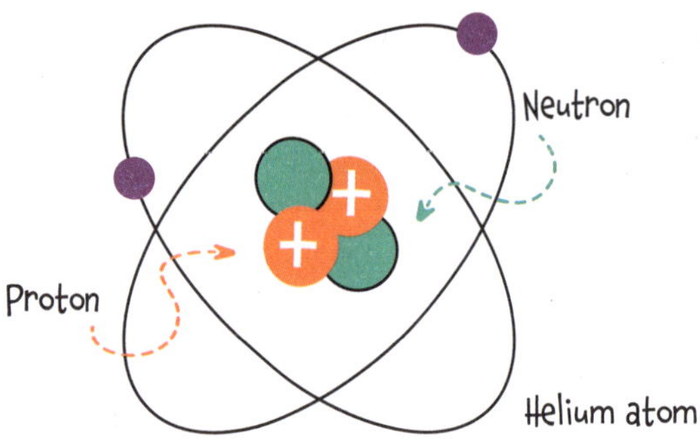

Fusing hydrogen

A hydrogen atom has just a single proton. A helium atom has two protons and also two neutrons. To get four particles in the nucleus, it needs four hydrogen atoms to fuse. Two of the protons need to change to neutrons. When a proton turns to a neutron, it loses a tiny particle called a positron.

Losing mass

A helium nucleus has 99.3 percent of the mass of four hydrogen nuclei; the other 0.7 percent is lost as energy—as heat, light, and other forms of electromagnetic radiation. So far, over 4.5 billion years, the Sun has lost about the mass of 95 Earths this way.

72 You weigh less on the Moon

Mass is a measure of an amount of matter, or "stuff," but weight is the force acting on mass as a result of gravity. The Moon has less mass than Earth, so its gravity is lower—its "pull" on you is less than the Earth's gravitational pull, so you'd weigh less than you do at home on Earth.

Your mass would be the same (you don't lose any of your matter by going to the Moon), but the Moon's gravity can't hold you as firmly as Earth's gravity can. The result is that you could bounce really high with very little effort.

73 The middle of a hurricane is completely calm

A hurricane is a whirling spiral of wind that can tear down buildings. But if you're in the very middle of a hurricane, called the "eye," you won't notice any wind at all. Unfortunately, you can't stay in the middle for long, as the whole wind system moves along.

Up, down, and around

A hurricane forms over the ocean when warm air near the surface of the sea rises. Warm air rises because it's less dense than cold air. The warm air carries water that has evaporated from the sea. As it goes up, it leaves a gap that colder air rushes to fill. Then that new air gets warm and wet and rises, too. As the air goes higher, it cools and the water forms little droplets making clouds. The clouds pile up into huge columns and wind begins blowing around them. Wind gathers the clouds into a circle with a space in the middle. That space will be the eye of the storm.

DID YOU KNOW?

A hurricane can be 1,600 km (1,000 mi) across and 16 km (10 mi) high! The eye is just 30–65 km (20–40 mi) across.

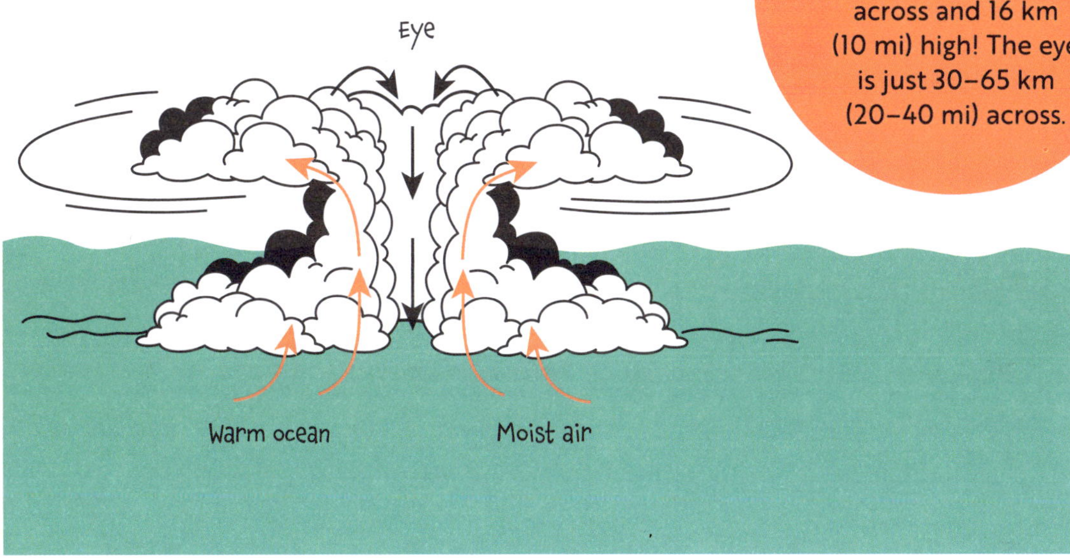

Eye, eye

Around the storm, hot air that rises and cools usually spills over the outside edge of the hurricane. It falls back to the sea where it might be pulled in to warm again. But a little of the air falls into the middle. This balances out the hot air rising. The result is a calm central space, where clouds aren't collecting and winds aren't raging.

74 A teaspoonful of neutron star weighs as much as Mount Everest

A neutron star is a star that has collapsed in on itself. It's the heaviest thing in the Universe, except for a black hole, and it contains lots of mass in a very small space. Just one teaspoonful would contain around a billion tons of matter.

Dead stars

A neutron star forms when a star much larger than the Sun collapses at the end of its life. It's the core left over from a supernova (see page 10). The original star might have had 10 to 25 times the mass of the Sun. The remaining neutron star has about 1.4 times the mass of the Sun—but it's crammed into a sphere only 10 km (6 mi) across, making it super-dense. (The rest of its mass has been blasted out into space.) This kind of compression is achieved by squeezing out almost all of the space between atoms.

Squashed flat

Because an object with a lot of mass has a strong gravitational pull, neutron stars have powerful gravity: 200 billion times the gravity we feel on Earth. That means that if you could land on a neutron star (you can't), you would be so powerfully attracted to the middle of it that your body would be entirely flattened. Gravity pulls equally on all parts of a surface—that's what makes planets roughly spherical—so you wouldn't be allowed to remain as a lump on the surface.

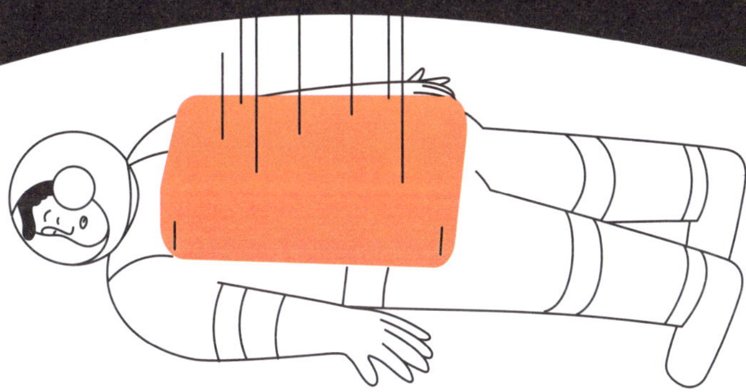

75 There could be a hidden planet

NASA scientists are looking for an extra planet near the edge of the solar system. They think it might be there because objects in the region act rather strangely.

Wonky belt

The Kuiper Belt is a wide band of space occupied by lots of rocky objects too small to count as planets, including Pluto. Some of these don't orbit the Sun in quite the way that astronomers would expect. Their odd orbits could be explained if they were being pulled off course by a really large object—a large planet, for example—out of view.

On the lookout

No one's ever seen this new planet, called Planet Nine, but using very powerful telescopes, astronomers will search the path of the orbit they think it follows. It will be hard to spot because it'll reflect very little sunlight so far from the Sun. But it can't hide forever!

Planet profile

Planet Nine would need to be about the same size as Neptune or Uranus to cause the disrupted orbits. It would be around 20 times farther from the Sun than Neptune, which would make its "year" between 10,000 and 20,000 years long. That means that the last time Planet Nine was where it is now in its orbit, humans had either just started farming or were still living in caves. It's a long time to wait for a birthday!

Glossary

Acid: A chemical compound that is soluble in water and tastes sour.

Acrylic: An artificial fabric.

Air resistance: A type of friction that slows an object's movement through the air.

Area: The space inside a two-dimensional shape.

Asteroid: A small rocky object made up of material left over from the birth of the solar system.

Astronomer: Someone who studies space and the objects in it.

Atmosphere: A layer of gases kept around a planet, star, or other object by its gravity.

Atom: The smallest possible particle of a chemical element.

Axis: An imaginary line around which an object rotates.

Big Bang: The start of the Universe with the instant appearance of a tiny, hot, dense point from which all matter and energy has expanded.

Black hole: A superdense point in space, usually formed by a collapsed core of a giant star. A black hole's gravity is so powerful that even light can't escape from it.

Buoyancy: A force that keeps objects floating in water.

Carbon dioxide: A waste gas produced by living things, made up of one carbon atom bonded to two oxygen atoms.

Chemical reaction: Two or more chemicals reacting together, making and breaking the chemicals' bonds.

Circuit: An electrical circuit is a closed loop, with electricity flowing round it.

Comet: A chunk of rock and ice from the edge of the solar system.

Compass: An instrument for finding directions. It consists of a magnetic pointer that always points north.

Condense: Change from a gas or vapor to a liquid.

Conductor: A substance that allows electricity or heat to flow through it.

Crystal: A special kind of solid where the atoms or molecules are arranged in a repeating pattern.

Current: The flow of electrons that produces electricity.

Dark energy: A mysterious form of energy that seems to push galaxies apart, making the Universe expand.

Dark matter: A strange, invisible substance that forms most of the mass in the Universe.

Decibel: A measure of the volume of sound.

Density: The weight of a substance compared to the amount of space it fills.

Diameter: The length of a straight line dividing a circle in half through the middle.

Displace: To take the place of something.

Drag: The force that slows an object moving through a gas or liquid.

Dwarf planet: A world orbiting a star that doesn't meet the conditions to be classed as a planet.

Electromagnetic radiation: Energy that travels as waves. The full range of electromagnetic radiation includes radio waves, microwaves, visible light, x-rays, and gamma ray radiation.

Electron: Tiny particle with a negative electrical charge. They are the smallest parts of atoms; the flow of electrons produces electricity.

Element: One of the 118 chemicals that cannot be broken down into simpler chemicals.

Energy: The power to perform work.

Equator: An imaginary line drawn around the middle of Earth.

Eruption: Molten rock (lava) and gases pouring from a volcano.

Evaporate: To turn from liquid into gas.

Freeze: To turn from liquid into a solid through getting cold.

Friction: A force that slows moving objects.

Fungi: Small organisms of the group that includes yeasts and mushrooms.

Galaxy: A large system of stars, gas, and dust with anything from millions to trillions of stars.

Gas: A substance that is like air and has no fixed shape.

Gravitational: Produced by gravity.

Gravity: A force that works between objects with mass, drawing them together.

Helium: A gas, the second lightest chemical element.

Hemisphere: Half of a sphere; a half of the earth, usually as divided into northern and southern halves, or hemispheres, by the equator; or into western and eastern halves by an imaginary line passing through the poles.

Horizon: The line that separates the sky from land or sea.

Hydrogen: A gas, the lightest chemical element.

Identical: Exactly the same.

Inertia: The tendency of matter to continue in its existing state, unless changed by some force.

Insulated: Protected to prevent electricity or heat escaping.

Kinetic energy: Energy possessed by an object while it's moving.

Kuiper Belt: A ring of lumps of rock and ice beyond the orbit of Neptune. Pluto is the largest-known Kuiper Belt Object.

Light year: The distance light travels in a year—about 9.5 trillion km (5.9 trillion mi).

Liquid: A substance that flows to fill the shape of a container or over a surface, like water.

Magnet: A material or object that produces a magnetic field.

Mass: A measure of how much matter there is in an object.

Microwave: Electromagnetic radiation with a shorter wavelength than visible light.

Milky Way: Our home galaxy. Our solar system is about 28,000 light years from the middle.

Molecule: The smallest possible unit of a substance that still behaves like that substance. A molecule is made up of two or more atoms.

Momentum: The tendency of an object to keep moving in the same direction unless changed by a force acting on it.

Neutron: A tiny particle with no electric charge in the middle of an atom.

Nucleus: The middle of an atom, made of protons and neutrons.

Orbit: A fixed path taken by one object in space around another because of the effect of gravity.

Organism: A living thing.

Oxygen: A gas that is essential for life.

Photon: The tiniest possible parcel of light energy.

Planet: A world orbiting a star that has enough mass and gravity to pull itself into a sphere, and clear space in its orbit of other large objects.

Pole: The end of a magnet, north or south, where its magnetic force is strongest.

Positron: A tiny particle equivalent to an electron but with a positive electric charge.

Potential energy: Energy in an object, such as heat in hot water or tension in a stretched balloon.

Pressure: The force of one object or substance pressing on another.

Proton: A tiny positively charged particle in the middle of an atom.

Radiation: A form of energy that travels as rays or waves. Radiation can travel through empty space.

Radioactivity: The process of emitting waves of energy or particles as atoms change

Ratio: A way of comparing two quantities, showing how much there is of each.

Red Dwarf: A small, faint star with a cool red surface and less than half the mass of the Sun.

Rotate: To turn around.

Solar System: The eight planets (including Earth) and their moons, and other objects such as asteroids, which orbit around the Sun.

Solar-powered: Driven by energy from sunlight.

Solid: A substance that keeps its size and shape.

Solidify: To become solid.

Spectrum: Full range of visible light, from red to violet, like a rainbow.

Sphere: An object shaped like a ball.

Static electricity: Electricity that collects on an object but does not immediately flow as a current.

Supernova: An enormous explosion marking the death of a star more massive than the Sun.

Telecommunications: Electronic methods of communication that work over a long distance, such as telephones, radio, TV, and the Internet.

Telescope: A tool that collects light or other radiation from space and uses it to create an image.

Temperature: The measure of heat.

Terminal: The end of a battery.

Trillion: A million million (1,000,000,000,000).

Vapor: Liquid suspended as tiny droplets, between the state of a liquid and a gas.

Vibrations: Tiny shaking movements.

Voltage: A measure of the "push" with which electricity is forced through a circuit. The higher the voltage, the more electricity is flowing.

Volume: Space occupied by a substance or object, or within a container.

Wavelength: The distance between the peak of one wave and the next.

Index